AF477525

COREPRESENTATION OF GRAMMATICAL STRUCTURE

CROOM HELM LINGUISTICS SERIES
edited by Roger Lass

ON CASE GRAMMAR
Prolegomena to a Theory of Grammatical Relations
John M. Anderson

DEFINITENESS AND INDEFINITENESS
John Hawkins

COREPRESENTATION OF GRAMMATICAL STRUCTURE

MICHAEL B. KAC

CROOM HELM LONDON

British Library Cataloguing in Publication Data

Kac, Michael B
    Corepresentation of grammatical strucutre.
    1. English language — Syntax
    I. Title
    425   PE1361

ISBN 0-85664-538-9

Printed in Great Britain by Biddles Ltd, Guildford, Surrey

CONTENTS

To E and W,
Joy and Comfort

ACKNOWLEDGMENTS

I wish to express my thanks to a number of friends and colleagues who have contributed in various ways to this study. First and foremost is Gerald Sanders, who kindly read and commented on an earlier draft, supplied much constructive criticism, and enabled me to substitute light for heat at many points in the presentation. Various ideas developed here first saw the light of day in conversations with Larry Hutchinson from which I have profited in ways too numerous to mention. In addition, I have had much valuable feedback from Linda Norman, Monika Former, Cheryl Arko, Justin Holl, Patrick O'Malley, and Anne Utschig; my thanks to them for everything from detecting careless mistakes to pointing out significant possibilities for substantive improvement. Needless to say, none of the foregoing bear any responsibility for errors that remain or for my own unwillingness to back down under fire from a cherished position.

Although it may not be obvious from the text itself, I feel that I owe an intellectual debt to Charles Fillmore, whose work is in part responsible for my beginning to think about the questions with which this study is concerned. In particular, his arguments in favor of structural representations employing labeled relations provided an important part of the initial impetus to explore a conception of grammatical analysis which turned ultimately into that developed here.

Finally, special thanks to the Graduate School of the University of Minnesota for financial support during the summer of 1973, when a first version of this study was committed to paper, and during the 1973-74 academic year, when a number of substantial revisions and modifications were undertaken. It is my hope that the return justifies this investment.

Minneapolis   Michael B. Kac
June 1975

PROSPECTUS

This study is concerned with some descriptive and explanatory problems
currently confronting the theory of generative grammar and presents an
approach to them in terms of a model called COREPRESENTATIONAL
GRAMMAR, henceforth 'CORG'. It will be argued that with regard to
these problems, CORG has significant substantive advantages over
transformational grammar ('TG').

The term 'corepresentational' derives from the assumption that the
grammatical structure of a sentence is simultaneously specified by two
representations of distinct formal types: a CATEGORIAL representation
(or constituent structure analysis) and a RELATIONAL representation
(which is here taken to be an unordered conjunction of statements
indicating abstract relations among grammatically significant elements).
The precise formal nature of these two modes is discussed in detail in
Chapter 1. For purposes of this study, 'relation' can be taken to mean
'grammatical relation' (e.g., Subject-of, Object-of), though of course
there are other types of abstract relations which must be recognized
in linguistic analysis (e.g., anaphoric relations such as coreference and
logical relations such as entailment). One goal of a corepresentational
description of a language is to provide precisely formulated principles
which will correctly determine for any arbitrarily selected and
categorially analyzed sentence of a language the grammatical relations
which obtain within it; it is this goal with which the present work is
principally concerned.

There are two major differences between CORG and TG. First
and foremost, CORG operates under the constraint that in so far as the
rules of grammar make reference to categorial structure, they refer
exclusively to SURFACE categorial structure. No abstract level of
categorial representation, such as 'deep' or 'underlying' structure, is
recognized. In this regard, CORG differs even from 'interpretive'
transformational models (such as that of Jackendoff 1972), which
hold that an abstract level of deep structure is necessary even though
some facets of semantic interpretation are determined by rules operating
on surface structure.[1] Second, in CORG the explicit provision of a
mode of relational representation permits the formulation of rules
which make direct reference to grammatical relations, whereas in TG
these may be referred to only indirectly (via reference to associated

sequential or configurational information). In this regard, CORG resembles relational grammar,[2] though the resemblance ends with this one shared similarity. Relational grammar makes crucial use of rules that are essentially translations of transformational rules, the difference being that whereas transformations change order and configuration, their analogues in relational grammar change grammatical relations. (An example of such a 'transrelational' rule, as Johnson calls them (1976), is the cognate of the passive transformation which consists in part of the instruction to convert Objects into Subjects.) In CORG, there is no mechanism for deriving one grammatical relation from another; accordingly, terms such as 'Subject' and 'Object' refer exclusively to LOGICAL Subject and Object, so that in an active-passive sentence pair such as *Harry likes Maxine/ Maxine is liked by Harry, Harry* is characterized as Subject of the verb in both. The status of the 'surface Subject' of passives is handled differently from the usual way — for details, see §2.4.[3]

Lest there be misunderstanding on this point, let it be said at the outset that this study will not, for the most part, be concerned with presenting new facts, nor will it argue for anything revolutionary in the way of a basic conception of linguistic structure. The phenomena to be discussed here are largely familiar (though this does not necessarily mean that they are well understood), and the fundamental assumptions are essentially those of traditional grammar. What is new is the way in which certain well-known phenomena will be interpreted theoretically and related to one another. There is also an important difference in emphasis between CORG and its generative forebears: In TG, the central questions pertain to the nature of underlying structures and of the rules required to map them into surface structures; accordingly, much stress is placed on the degree of difference between the two kinds of structure and on the formal properties of transformational rules. In CORG, the principal issue is perceived rather differently, namely, as pertaining to the discovery of regularities in the manner in which abstract relational information is encoded by sentences. This in turn means that surface structure must be the main object of attention. The main question to which we are addressed is: To what structural information about a sentence must a language user have access in order to determine correctly its abstract relational content? TG, at least in practice, has given this question marginal attention at best, though there can hardly be any doubt as to its importance or interest.[4]

The data in this study are drawn primarily from English, though it is hoped that the resulting hypotheses will have cross-linguistic validity. In any event, careful description of individual languages is a necessary first step in defining the issues which must be faced in constructing a theory of grammar with universal or near-universal scope.

The presentation is organized as follows:

Chapter 1 outlines the basics of corepresentational theory and presents an initial comparison with TG. Chapter 2 then develops and defends a specific set of principles for the analysis of simplex sentences in English. One of these principles, the 'Oblique Distance Condition', provides another comparison point with TG, and an argument is presented to the effect that the generalization expressed by this principle strengthens the case in favor of CORG.

Chapter 3, the first of three concerned with complex sentences, deals with complementation. Three major topics are taken up, namely, the determination of the predicational structure of complement constructions, the treatment of discontinuous argument-predicate dependencies in such constructions, and the behavior of complementizers. The apparatus developed is defended on the grounds that there are constructions whose behavior can be explained in a corepresentational treatment but not in a transformational one.

Chapters 4 and 5 deal with the phenomena usually accounted for in transformational theory by the Complex NP and Coordinate Structure Constraints (Ross 1967). It is argued that these constraints (and the general theoretical framework within which they are couched) are nonexplanatory but that at least a minimal level of explanatory adequacy can be achieved given a corepresentational model. It is shown first that certain restrictions must be imposed on the manner in which predicational structure is assigned to well-formed sentences containing complex NP's or coordinations; given these restrictions, it follows automatically that structures which violate the Complex NP or Coordinate Structure Constraint will be ill-formed, since they must be analyzed as containing predications that violate other principles of the theory. Thus the facts motivating these constraints are a consequence, given the corepresentational approach, of general principles which govern predicational structure and which would be required in any case.

The concluding chapter, Chapter 6, seeks to place the results of this study in a broader metatheoretical context. Certain objections are anticipated and discussed, and the question of the relationship of linguistic and psychological theories is considered. Finally, it is argued

that the advantages of CORG over TG are a consequence of a
'notionalist' or 'conceptualist' viewpoint taken by the former, as
opposed to the 'formalist' viewpoint of the latter.

Although CORG is conceived of as an alternative to TG, it
is none the less important to emphasize that the two theories have
some significant properties in common. For one thing, both are
generative in orientation in the sense that both seek to provide
a finite set of principles for the characterization of essential
properties of the members of an infinitely large set of linguistic
objects. Moreover, both derive their impetus from the conviction
that formal rigour is essential to linguistic description. The claim
by Chomsky (1957, p. 5) that 'precisely constructed models of
linguistic structure can play an important role, both negative and
positive, in the process of discovery itself' is taken here as an
indispensable premise. Though a measure of polemic is inevitable
in a work of this sort, it must not be allowed to obscure the fact
that no new approach can completely escape indebtedness to what
preceded it; the present case is certainly no exception. If my conclusions are correct, this can only enhance the value of the method
of inquiry associated with the generative grammatical tradition.

Notes

1. Although interpretive semantics takes a rather narrow view of what may be
   accomplished by transformations, it does not represent a fundamental
   challenge to the basic assumptions underlying TG. The impetus for the
   development of the interpretive model comes from the desire to limit
   transformations and the structures interrelated thereby to a purely
   'syntactic' function; thus, semantic considerations are not valid in
   motivating them. Jackendoff (1972) assumes that there is other than
   semantic motivation for abstract deep structures and that these are the
   natural inputs to the portion of the semantic component which
   determines predicate-argument relations. But 'assumes' is to be taken
   literally here: he provides no defense of either claim. He also relies
   crucially on such notions as 'transformational cycle' and on the
   intermediate structures of transformational derivations.
2. This term refers to a model suggested by D. Perlmutter and P. Postal,
   but not yet developed by them in print; a closely related model is given
   a detailed presentation in Johnson 1976. A proposal to incorporate
   direct reference to grammatical relations in the statements of certain
   kinds of rules is made in Kac (1972a) and is justified on much the same
   sorts of grounds as those employed by Johnson. Yet another approach
   having some points in common with CORG is currently under investigation by Derwing, Prideaux, and Baker and their associates at the
   University of Alberta; I would like to express my thanks to Gary
   Prideaux for providing me with a preview of this work.

3. Another example of a transrelational rule is the analogue of the transformation of Subject Raising, consisting in the instruction to convert the Subject of a predicate into an Object of the immediately superordinate predicate. For an alternative analysis, see Kac 1976a.
4. Something like this issue does arise in connection with work on 'perceptual strategies' for reconstructing deep structures given their surface reflexes. But the tendency is to treat the problem as one pertaining to 'performance' and hence as of only ancillary relevance to the study of grammar. See §6.2.1 for further discussion.

1 / FUNDAMENTAL PRINCIPLES

1.1. Corepresentation Defined

Grammatical theory since antiquity has recognized that there are two modes of representation of the grammatical structure of a sentence. The first, which we may call CATEGORIAL, involves a segmentation of the sentence into constituents and the identification of each constituent as a member of one of a finite set of categories such as 'noun', 'verb', 'noun phrase', and so on. A graphic display such as a labelled bracketing or tree ('P-marker') may be regarded as specifying the categorial structure of the sentence with which it is associated.[1] Henceforth we will refer to any such structural description as a CATEGORIAL REPRESENTATION.

The second mode of representation is RELATIONAL. As the term implies, a description in this mode identifies relations among elements (e.g., the grammatical relation 'Subject-of' or the anaphoric relation 'is coreferential with'). A RELATIONAL REPRESENTATION[2] will henceforth be construed as consisting of a conjunction of statements s_1 & s_2 & . . . & s_n where each s is of the form

    (1) $X = \rho(Y)$

which is read as 'X bears the relation ρ to Y' or 'X is the/a ρ of Y'.[3] For example, the English sentence

    (2)   Harry likes vodka.

may be presumed to have the relational representation

    (3)   *Harry* = SUBJ*(like)* & *vodka* = OBJ*(like)*.

where the labels SUBJ/OBJ and the terms 'Subject/Object' will henceforth be taken to refer exclusively to the relations LOGICAL SUBJECT and LOGICAL OBJECT. We will say that a categorial and a relational representation COREPRESENT the grammatical structure of a sentence with which they are associated; any such pairing of a categorial and relational representation is thus a COREPRESENTATION.

Strictly speaking, of course, a categorial representation has relational content as well. More precisely, such a representation is a graphic display of a type of structure expressible in terms of such relations as 'is a', 'dominates', 'precedes', 'commands', and so on. These relations may be called 'geometric' or 'formal', whereas a relation like SUBJ might be called 'notional'. Thus, 'relational representation' really means 'notional relational representation', and 'categorial representation' means 'geometric relational representation' where one of the geometric relations involved happens to be the CATEGORY IDENTIFICATION RELATION 'is a'.

In its broadest sense, the term 'corepresentational grammar' refers to any approach to linguistic description which, explicitly or or implicitly, associates relational (notional) characterizations with categorially (geometrically) analyzed sentences. Given such a broad definition, virtually every theory of grammar ever seriously proposed is corepresentational — including TG. We will, however, define the term more narrowly, as denoting a theory which (a) assumes only one level of categorial structure (i.e., surface structure) and (b) assumes exlicitly that relational structure is described formally via such representations as (3) or via some clearly equivalent formalism. Some specific arguments in favor of this formalism will be presented below.

1.2. Generation of Corepresentations

The core of a corepresentational description of a language is a set of axioms on the basis of which it is possible to prove as theorems all true statements of the form 'Sentence S with categorial representation K has relational representation R' and no false statements of this form. The sense in which CORG is a model for generative grammatical description should thus be clear: There must be finitely many axioms, formalized to the point where their consequences can be unequivocally determined, and from which infinitely many statements of the type just described can be derived. It is important to note, however, that axiomatization of this type does not — and need not — define an algorithm for generating corepresentations (i.e., a mechanical procedure for mapping between categorial and relational structures). The requirement that a generative grammar of a language be construed as an algorithm, though widely assumed, seems needlessly strong; we will require here only that all and only the set of true statements connecting categorially analyzed sentences with their relational representations be deducible from the principles of the theory according to accepted rules of logical inference, whether or not there is always a mechanical step-by-step method for doing so.

The axioms for a given language will obviously have to include at least a set of lexical entries and a phrase structure grammar of some sort as well. These will be discussed later in the chapter. For the moment, we will focus on the principles involved in associating categorial and relational representations, principles which are of three major types:

(a) RULES OF COREPRESENTATION ('C-rules'), defined as language-specific conditions involved in determining the relational structure of categorially analyzed sentences. Each such rule associates some specific item of relational information with a sentence on the basis of some specific item of other information about the sentence.

(b) METACONDITIONS, defined as UNIVERSAL principles which govern the internal structure of predications and which jointly define for all languages the notion 'possible corepresentation'.

(c) DOMAIN RESTRICTIONS, defined as principles which in complex sentences identify the structural units that can be taken as representing the predications of which the sentence is constituted.

In addition, there are various miscellaneous principles pertaining to the interpretation and interaction of the components of the theory.

Chapters 2-5 develop and justify a system of C-rules, metaconditions, and domain restrictions for simplex and complex sentences of English. The remainder of this chapter is devoted to filling in certain further details to clarify the outlines of the corepresentational model.

1.3. On Comparing Approaches

I digress briefly at this early point to comment on the basis for comparison of CORG and TG. In regard to the scope and limits of such comparison, two major points must be made:

First, there is one level at which it is meaningless to compare CORG and TG, since at this level they do not represent different approaches. The reason is that the term 'transformational' is subject to so loose a construal that it applies to any formal model of grammatical description which aims at a reasonable degree of comprehensiveness and generality. Just as all grammars are corepresentational on the basis of a sufficiently loose definition of this term, so are all grammars transformational in that they must map between differing kinds of structural representations of linguistic objects in accordance with some set of explicitly formulated principles. Thus it makes no sense to compare CORG and TG in the abstract; rather, we must compare a particular transformational model and a particular corepresentational model. The reference of 'CORG' and 'TG' will thus be particularized for our purposes as follows: The referent of the former will be the theory presented in this study; the referent of the latter, while heterodox and amorphous in character, can none the less be seen in its outlines in the classic works of the generative syntactic literature since 1957.

Second, CORG and TG represent not so much different HYPOTHESES about the nature of grammatical systems as different METALANGUAGES within which to frame such hypotheses. Comparison of these meta-languages is based at least as much on methodological considerations as on empirical ones; whereas the same principles may be expressible in either, one is none the less preferable in that its particular points of emphasis lead to a more revealing characterization of problems and thus to more rapid and extensive discovery of viable and interesting hypotheses. I am therefore not challenging TG with regard to its capacity to 'account for the facts' (since, among other things, any analytic paradigm may be made to account for anything given a sufficient degree of ad hoc embellishment), but rather I am questioning the KIND of account provided on the basis of considerations of generality, natural-ness, and explanatory power. My claim is that CORG is preferable to TG on all three counts, at least with respect to the problems to be considered in this study.

1.4. Properties and Functions of Relational Representation

An important phenomenon of natural language is the RELATIONAL EQUIVALENCE of certain categorially distinct structures. For example, notice that

(4)   a. Harry likes vodka.
       b. Vodka is liked by Harry.
       c. Vodka, Harry likes.

all have the same relational structure — that specified in (3) above. (Recall that SUBJ and OBJ are here construed as Logical Subject/Object; consequently, *Harry* is SUBJ *(like)* in both (4a) and 4(b).) A related phenomenon may be observed in a paradigm such as

(5)   a. It's vodka that Fred knows Harry likes.
       b. Vodka, which Harry likes, is drunk in Russia.
       c. Harry wanted to like vodka.

d. Liking vodka upset Harry.

The relational representations of these sentences, whatever their differences, all properly include (3), despite the fact that *Harry, vodka,* and *like* occur in different categorial configurations in each. It is precisely such facts as these that provided the initial motivation for the development of TG, and TG derives a significant amount of its support from the relative lack of transparency of surface structures relative to the underlying grammatico-semantic relations obtaining in the sentences with which they are associated. Much early work by advocates of TG was concerned with showing the inadequacies and limitations of the surface-oriented analytic techniques that characterized much (if not all) of structuralist syntax; but as we shall see, transformations do not constitute the only — or even the best — theoretical device for approaching the problems in question.

The transformational strategy for dealing with (4-5) and parallel cases would be to specify a single categorial configuration at a more abstract level of analysis, within which *Harry, like,* and *vodka* would occur; a set of transformations would then be given with the function of deforming this configuration in such a way as to derive all the surface variants. In CORG, however, the strategy is different: Rather than assume a more abstract categorial structure underlying all members of a set of relationally equivalent surface configurations, we make only the assumption that to the extent that distinct surface structures are relationally equivalent, their relational representations must be identical. So, for example, we do not derive the sentences in (4) from a common underlying categorial structure; rather, we posit a set of principles which will jointly predict (3) as the relational representation of each surface variant. Similarly, we do not assume that the sentences in (5) derive from categorial structures containing *Harry, like,* and *vodka* in some single subconfiguration but rather seek to predict (3) as a subpart of the relational representations of these various sentences. As we will see in the succeeding chapters, the common relational properties of these seven example sentences can be exposed on the basis of quite general principles, given certain assumptions about how a grammar should be constructed.

Formally, a relational representation differs from a surface categorial representation in two fundamental respects: A relational representation is UNORDERED (i.e., s_i & s_j expresses exactly the same information as s_j & s_i where $s_{i,j}$ are statements of the form (1)) and UNHIERARCHIZED (i.e., the '&' connective is associative).[4]

As a preliminary illustration of the corepresentational strategy, let us examine the familiar case of the active-passive relation in English. In his discussion of this phenomenon, Chomsky (1957) made much of the fact that in sentence pairs of the form

(6) a. NP_1-V-NP_2
     b. NP_2-BE-V-EN-*by*-NP_1

identical selectional restrictions must be imposed by V on the two NP s regardless of their order relative to each other. Without a rule to specifically relate active and corresponding passive, he argued, the restriction imposed by V on NP_1 would have to be stated twice, once for the order NP_1-V and again for the order V- . . . NP_1 ; an analogous situation obtains for the restriction imposed by V on NP_2. This duplication can be eliminated, however, if one order is taken as 'primitive' or 'basic', selectional restrictions are stated relative to the basic order, and all other orders are then derived from the basic order by operations which by definition preserve co-occurrence relations. This argument form has been used again and again to justify particular transformations, both in the research literature and in textbooks.

From a corepresentational viewpoint, however, this classic argument is not compelling. Notice that it depends crucially on the assumption that selectional restrictions make necessary reference to the relative order of constituents; but there is no reason for such an assumption, and it is not made in CORG. Rather, it is assumed that selectional restrictions refer to predicate-argument relations such as SUBJ or OBJ. Each such restriction may be viewed as a statement of the form

(7)   Any NP instantiating X in a relational statement

       $X = a(P)$ must bear the feature [F] .

where a is a predicate-argument relation and P a predicate. For example,

(8)   Any NP instantiating X in a relational statement

       $X = SUBJ$ *(like)* must bear the feature [+ANIMATE] .

For any selectional restriction imposed by P on $a(P)$, that restriction is satisfied iff the NP analyzed as $a(P)$ bears the feature named in the restriction; to determine whether such a restriction is satisfied in a given case, it is sufficient to locate $a(P)$ in the relational representation and to check the inherent features of the NP so analyzed. As long as there is a way of associating the same relational representation with active and corresponding passive, and selectional restrictions take the form of (7) above, there is no motivation on grounds of co-occurrence equivalence for positing rules which derive one categorial structure from another.

None the less, the significance of the difference between CORG and TG remains open to question: Is it really one of substance or merely of niceties? I suggest that there are genuinely substantive matters at stake — a position the support of which is one goal of this entire study and of which a detailed defense requires that the mechanics of the theory of corepresentational grammar be presented in detail. Certain items in support of the corepresentational position may, however, be presented even at this early point in the discussion.

The 'classical' transformationalist view is that the underlying categorial structures have both an ordering and a hierarchical structure. Let us consider first the position that underlying representations are ordered. Such a view is clearly entailed by the assumption that selectional restrictions are defined relative to particular orderings of elements; and this in turn raises the problem of deciding in particular cases (as in that of the English active-passive correspondence) what the basic order is to be taken to be. This turns out to be a highly problematical matter, as the recent literature on the subject attests.[5] But the issue, even if it could be resolved, is something of a red herring. There is no important theoretical consequence that would ensue from such a resolution; the entire question has assumed the importance it has, I would claim, solely because of the working assumptions of classical transformationalism. If one makes these assumptions, then a non-arbitrary basis is needed for certain decisions; but whether one decision or another is made is of importance only within the parochial confines of the theory — no important question about the nature of language hangs in the balance while the issue of underlying constituent order goes unsettled.[6]

The assumption that underlying representations are ordered has in fact been abandoned by some transformationalists (see, for example, Sanders 1970, Hudson 1972) in favour of the view that only hierarchical structure is imposed at the underlying level. It is therefore important to ask whether CORG and TG turn out to be essentially equivalent once the matter of ordering constituents in underlying P-markers is set aside. I maintain that the answer is negative, though it is necessary to go outside English to show that this is the case. I would like, therefore, briefly to examine a phenomenon which, in my view, clearly distinguishes the two approaches: gender agreement of adjectives in French.

As an initial but uncontroversial assumption, we take for granted that the relation Subject holds between the italicized N and the adjective in each of the following:

(9) a. Le *garçon* est *petit*. 'The boy is small'
 b. La *fille* est *petite*. 'The girl is small'
 c. le *petit garçon* 'the small boy'
 d. la *petite fille* 'the small girl'

We will call the adjectives in (9a-b) 'postverbal' and those in (9c-d) 'adnominal'. Adnominal adjectives in French vary as to whether they adopt pre- or postnominal position; *petit* occurs only prenominally, whereas the usual position for adnominal adjectives is postnominal. A peculiar case is the adjective *ancien,* meaning both 'ancient' and 'former' and taking different adnominal positions depending on the sense:

(10) a. l'ancien maître 'the former teacher (male)'
 b. l'ancienne maîtresse 'the former teacher (female)'
 c. le maître ancien $\Big\}$ 'the ancient teacher'
 d. la maîtresse ancienne

As can be seen, the adjective manifests gender agreement with the head noun regardless of sense or position in the adnominal construction. The following sentences show *ancien* in postverbal position:

(11) a. Le maître est ancien.
 b. La maîtresse est ancienne.

These two sentences translate only as 'The teacher is ancient'; '*The teacher is former' is impossible in French just as it is. in English.

It seems reasonable to regard *ancien* as a manifestation of two adjectives rather than one; let us henceforth use *ancien$_f$* to denote the adjective meaning 'former' and *ancien$_a$* to denote the adjective meaning 'ancient' The facts may then be summarized as follows:

(a) *ancien$_a$* occurs both postverbally and adnominally, taking postnominal position in the latter case.

(b) *ancien$_f$* occurs only prenominally, never postnominally or postverbally.

Let us now consider, from a transformational viewpoint, the problem of generating NPs such as (10a-b). There are two alternatives: The first and most natural from a distributional point of view would be to suppose that *ancien$_f$* occurs prenominally in underlying structure. The second alternative, less natural from this standpoint, would be to derive such NPs from underlying structures of the form

(12)

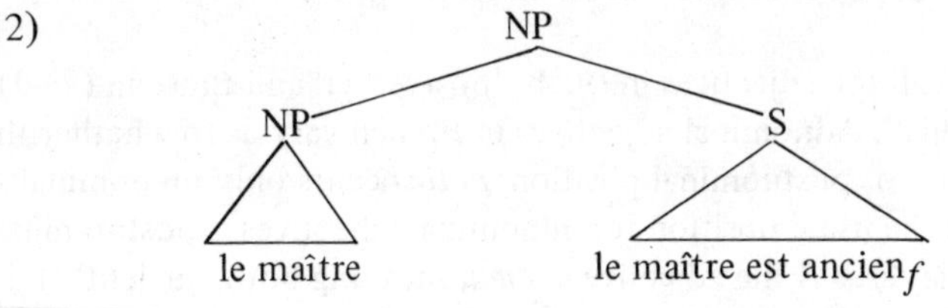

and to make Adjective Preposing obligatory for this and similar adjectives. Both approaches are descriptively adequate, and both are consistent with the exceptional nature of the item in question since regardless of which we choose, there must be some device to prevent it from surfacing in postverbal position. Thus it must either be marked $[-V\text{___}]$ (first alternative) or [+ADJECTIVE PREPOSING] (second alternative).

At this point we face a dilemma. Since there is no direct evidence for the existence of NPs like (12), due to the nature of the embedded S, we would be inclined to favor the first alternative over the second. Unfortunately, however, we then lose the possibility of a unitary treatment of gender agreement, since under the first alternative we need two different agreement rules — one for postverbal adjectives and another for adnominal ones. Notice, moreover, that this will be the case regardless of whether we take underlying P-markers to be ordered: assuming unordered base structures, one agreement rule must nonetheless make reference to the configuration $[_N A, N]$ and another to the configuration $[_S . . ., N, [_{VP} V, A]]$ (where ',' indicates unordered concatenation). In short, having two underlying positions for adjectives, while distributionally natural, interferes with a unitary account of the process of agreement; on the other hand, the generalization of the rule accounting for agreement can be accomplished only if we resort to such artefacts as (12). TG, of course, relies extensively on such fictitious structures — often on precisely the same kind of grounds as those just given for preferring the second alternative with regard to accounting for the distribution of *ancien$_f$*. But this is exactly the point: The fact that TG can capture certain generalizations only if recourse is allowed to such fictions is not an argument in favor of the fictions; it is an argument against TG.

In a corepresentational framework, however, there is no such dilemma. Since there is only one level of categorial structure, surface structure, fictions like (12) are excluded in principle; but a single agreement rule for adjectives can still be provided, since whether or not an adjective occurs adnominally, it agrees with the nominal bearing the relation SUBJ to it. Thus both (9a) and (9c), for example, have associated with them the relational statement

(13) *garçon* = SUBJ *(petit)*

The agreement rule is as follows:

(14) Any A instantiating X in a statement N = SUBJ (X)
      must bear the feature [a FEMININE] if N bears the
      feature [a FEMININE].

(This rule of course depends on information provided elsewhere in the grammar indicating that *petit* is [−FEMININE] and *petite* [+FEMININE] in order to be able to handle (9a,c).) For the cases with *ancien* the situation is similar; whether or not the adjective occurs adnominally, its Subject will be identified in the relational representation of the sentence in which it occurs, and rule (14) will be applicable. The correct generalization can therefore be maintained without requiring the generation of non-occurring categorial structures. This in turn suggests that at least insofar as the phenomenon of gender agreement is concerned, the more natural assumption is that the appropriate formulation of the required rule refers to relational representations in our sense rather than to P-markers — even if the latter are unordered. Before claiming unequivocally that this is so, however, let us consider one further possibility: Suppose one attempted within an unordered base theory of TG to achieve the same result as was attained with rule (14) with the following:

$$(15) \quad \begin{bmatrix} N \\ a \text{ FEMININE} \end{bmatrix}, X, A \text{ ====>} 1\ 2 \quad \begin{bmatrix} 3 \\ a \text{ FEMININE} \end{bmatrix}$$

$$1 \qquad\qquad 2 \quad 3$$

If (15) turns out to be equivalent to (14), then there is really no difference between a corepresentational treatment and a transformational one with unordered base structures, since (15) will apply regardless of the relative configuration of adjective and noun. But (15) is not equivalent to (14): (15) states that given ANY N and A in a sentence, the latter will agree with the former; but this is untrue. Adjectives agree only with certain nouns in the sentences in which they occur, and not with others: thus the X variable in (15) would have to be constrained in some way. The end result would be to impose a condition on (15) such that it may apply only when 1 and 3 are in particular configurations relative to each other — specifically, $[_N\ 1, 3]$ and $[_S \ldots, 1\ [_{VP}\ V, 3]]$. The addition of such a condition has the effect of restoring the original situation in which agreement must be accounted for with reference to two distinct configurations; and, of course, these two are just those in which the Subject relation holds between N and A.

The conclusion thus seems to be (a) that CORG and TG are substantively different on this point and (b) that CORG is preferable by virtue of the specific formal properties associated with relational as contrasted with underlying categorial representation.

1.5. Predicational Structure

In a sentence with more than one predicate, the structural description must indicate what the predications are as well as specifying the internal structure of each. For example, consider a sentence such as

(16) Fred knows Harry likes vodka.

Here there are two predications, one manifested by the sentence as a whole, the other by the embedded clause, which in turn acts as OBJ *(know)*. Let the notation 'Pr/P' denote 'predication whose predicate is P'; then the relational representation of (16) may be given as

(17)   *Fred* = SUBJ*(know)* & Pr/*like* = OBJ*(know)* & Harry = SUBJ*(like)* & *vodka* = OBJ*(like)*

Such a representation exhibits predicational structure as well; the content of Pr/*like* is specified by the last two conjuncts of the representation, that of Pr/*know* by the first two. Representation (17) is also associated with

(18)   Vodka, Fred knows Harry likes.

We will see in Chapter 3 that the equivalence of (16) and (18) can be accounted for in a revealing way without transformations; indeed, we will see that the relational structure of the latter is determined by almost exactly the same principles as those which assign a relational representation to the former — despite the fact that (18) contains a discontinuous complement and (16) does not.

1.6. Lexical Information

We will assume here that the lexicon in a corepresentational description of a language indicates both selectional restrictions and strict subcategorization of predicates. A schema for representing the former has already been introduced in §1.4; we will therefore confine ourselves here to discussion of the latter.

In the 'standard theory' of TG, the strict subcategorization of predicates is indicated by so-called contextual features that specify the categorial environment in which a predicate may appear at the underlying level. If a language is presumed to have underlying SVO order, then a verb may be specified as transitive via the feature [+___NP], to cite a standard illustrative example. Since CORG has no underlying categorial level, however, some alternative strategy must be adopted. One possibility is to classify predicates as to 'placedness', i.e., as to the number of distinct arguments required by predicates: intransitive predicates are 'one-place', predicates requiring both Subject and Object are 'two-place', and so on. A second alternative, perhaps more transparent, is to mark predicates for the kinds of arguments that they take. For example, let a, β be distinct predicate-argument relations and let P be a two-place predicate taking an a and a β; we could then associate with this predicate the feature $[+ *a, + *\beta]$, where $[+ *\rho]$ is interpreted as expressing the information 'requires an argument in relation ρ'. As a concrete example, consider *hit,* which would be $[+ * \text{SUBJ}, + * \text{OBJ}]$, or *give,* which would be [+ * SUBJ, + * OBJ, + * DATIVE] . (Actually, because of other features of the CORG framework, no predicate need be marked in the lexicon as [+ * SUBJ] ; see §2.2 for details.)

Empirically, there seems to be no particular reason for making one choice over the other, and no decision between alternatives will be argued for here. There are, however, reasons for regarding either as superior to the approach adopted in the standard theory of TG. Consider the fact that transitivity is predictable on the basis of other information: for example, a predicate having essentially the meaning of the English verb *hit* will, by virtue of being an 'interactional' verb, necessarily be two-place. It thus seems reasonable to suppose that there is a universal redundancy rule which associates transitivity with all predicates marked [+INTERACTIONAL] ; but there is no guarantee that a rule [+INTERACTIONAL] --> [+ __NP] can be universal, since it is not at all evident that SVO underlying order – or ANY order for that matter – can be taken as universal. This in turn suggests that order-based strict subcategorization features are suspect.

1.7. Generation of Categorial Structures

We now take up the question of the means by which categorial structures are assigned to sentences. One component of the surface structure generator required in a corepresentational description is a set of phrase structure rules. Clearly, if there are no transformations, then these PS-rules will have to be 'comprehensive' in the sense that they will have to account directly for all types of surface constituency. An advocate of TG might well argue that a transformational approach is therefore preferable, since it allows for a much simpler phrase structure component; that is, the PS-rules generate only a small subset of the total set of P-markers, the remainder being derived by transformations. Two points must be made in responding to this claim:

(a) First, observe that maintenance of a restricted set of PS-rules is viable only if certain other conditions obtain. No matter how much the PS-rules may be simplified, the simplification has to be paid for elsewhere by the incorporation of transformations to account for structures not generated in the base. There is some point in proceeding this way if the transformations have other motivation, as indeed they are presumed to. In particular, since the transformations play a role with regard to the 'relating function' of a grammar (i.e., since they account for certain types of equivalence among distinct surface structures such as relational equivalence), it would appear that TG can neatly kill two birds with one stone by having part of the constituent structure generating function of the grammar absorbed by rules which also fulfil the relating function. This in turn presupposes that transformations represent the optimal means of fulfilling the relating function of a generative grammar; but this, as will be argued in the next four chapters, is anything but a foregone conclusion.

(b) Second, consider the constituent structure generating function itself. In order to fulfil this function, every transformation must be analyzed as a sequence of so-called 'elementary transformations', each of which has a specified effect on constituent structure. (For example, transformations which move or introduce elements must specify the superordinate node to which the moved or added element is to be attached; the elementary transformations of 'sister adjunction' and 'Chomsky adjunction' are intended to serve this purpose.) It is thus assumed that there are TWO distinct formal mechanisms for the assignment of constituent structure: PS-rules for the assignment of such structure to base strings and elementary transformations for the assignment of this structure to transforms. I have suggested elsewhere (Kac 1972b) that this is a peculiar assumption, and I have proposed that the single function of determining constituent structure be fulfilled by a single formal mechanism, that of PS-rules. Regardless of the merits of this position, there appears to be no inherent advantage in the transformational approach, since while it does cut down on the number of PS-rules needed in a grammar, it does so at the cost of introducing a second mechanism (the theory of elementary transformations for the assignment of constituent structure) and thus leads to a model that is conceptually more complex than one which makes use of only one mechanism for this purpose. Within a transformational framework, one can achieve a conceptual simplification by eliminating the theory of elementary transformations and adopting a model in which constituent structure is assigned to transforms by 'recycling' them through the phrase structure component after the operation of each transformation. In at least one kind of case, where node labels are changed or new labels introduced (e.g., in the case of nominalization transformations), this would appear to be the preferred alternative in any event. Thus, the requirement that the phrase structure rules in a corepresentational description must be comprehensive cannot by itself be taken as militating against CORG and in favor of TG.

The surface structure generator for a corepresentational grammar will also have to incorporate devices for context-sensitivity; this might be done by including filtering templates of the type proposed by

Perlmutter (1971), though no doubt various other devices could be conceived. Without making a commitment to any particular mechanism at this point, I would like to emphasize that whatever one is chosen, its function is conceived as being limited to that of accounting for those restrictions not formulable in terms of the apparatus for generating corepresentations. For example, it seems reasonable to suppose that the constraints on the form of the verb-particle construction in English, and on the auxiliary-affix dependency (to cite two well-known instances) are restrictions on categorial structure alone rather than on pairings of categorial and relational representations; on the other hand, there are many cases where ill-formed sentences generable in principle by the simplest surface structure generator can none the less be filtered out on the basis of principles relating jointly to categorial and relational structure. It is with such cases that this study is princip-ally concerned.

It was noted earlier in the chapter (note 1) that our categorial representations will not be given in the form of trees, since we are eliminating the category S and hence the notion 'root node'. The reasons for taking this step cannot be made clear until a rather con-siderable amount of theoretical apparatus has been developed, but a hint can at least be given at this early stage. It turns out that there are some facts about complement constructions which cannot adequately be accounted for if the relations of subordination and superordination that must be taken into account in analyzing such constructions are taken to be exhibited by patterns of embedding of S's in trees. A completely new approach to the problem of representing subordinating structure must be adopted, which requires that the P-markers exhibiting the categorial structures of sentences not be trees. Accordingly, a sentence such as

(19) Harry knew Fed liked vodka.

would be represented categorially as follows:

(20)   NP   V   NP   V   NP
              | | | | |
            #Harry knew Fred liked vodka #

The relationship of Pr/*like* to Pr/*know,* i.e., that the former is sub-ordinate to the latter (the notion 'subordinate to' will be given a precise interpretation in Chapter 3), is determined via domain restrictions (see §1.2) which make reference to structural information provided by the operation of C-rules. (The relevant argumentation is to be found in §3.2.4.)

This result leaves us with a problem: If we have no S-nodes in P-markers, then we have no rule for expanding S; but this rule would seem essential to account for certain restrictions on well-formedness, i.e., those restrictions that determine how lower-order constituents may combine to form S-size units. For example, suppose that in some language there is a strict requirement that VPs are always second within the clause (so that there are no clauses of the form VP-NP). The rule S $-->$ NP-VP would account for such a restriction; in general, a string of lower-order constituents would be taken as categorially well-formed if it 'computes to S' given the S-expansion rule of the phrase structure component. Having given up such a rule, we must devise some alternative mechanism for handling the relevant facts. I raise the point here only to call attention to it; the specific approach to be taken will be described in §3.2.4 after the justification for the elimination of S has been dealt with.

Notes

1. For reasons to be presented in §3.2.4 we will actually represent categorial structures in a slightly different way, via branching diagrams or labelled bracketings without root nodes and without VP-nodes; thus, we will have representations such as

$$
\begin{array}{ccccc}
& \text{NP} & & & \text{NP} \\
& \wedge & & & \wedge \\
\text{ART} & \text{N} & \text{V} & \text{ART} & \text{N} \\
| & | & | & | & | \\
\text{The} & \text{man} & \text{saw} & \text{the} & \text{boy}
\end{array}
$$

2. The notion of relational representation employed here is essentially that proposed in Kac 1972a.
3. In general, X and Y will be overt elements of the categorially analyzed structure with which the relational representation is paired; there is one exception, however, involving 'recovered' elements (such as the second person Subject of a truncated imperative), which may instantiate X even though they do not occur overtly.
4. Some transformational models allow underlying categorial representations to be unordered.
5. For example, Peters (1970) discusses a paradox involving German, which may be analyzed as having either SVO or SOV order in underlying structure. Attempts to resolve the issue one way or the other, e.g. by Emonds (1970), Ross (1971), and Bach (1971), come to conflicting conclusions. With respect to English, there is debate over the hypothesis that

the underlying order should be presumed to be VSO. In many studies entirely arbitrary decisions are made as to which of several possible orders to take as underlying.

6. The issue can, of course, be finessed by abandonment of the notion that any decision has to be made. On the face of it, there is no compelling reason why it should not be assumed that a language can be validly analyzed as having more than one descriptively adequate grammar and that no decision need be made among the alternatives if clear justification is lacking for one over the others. The question of whether a language can be taken to have more than one possible underlying order of constituents is significant only if it is assumed that the notion 'underlying order of constituents' is itself theoretically valid. At present, there is no evidence that this is so.

2 ANALYSIS OF ENGLISH SIMPLEX SENTENCES

2.1 Active Constructions: Preliminary Approach

To begin the detailed presentation of the principles for generating corepresentations, I set a modest descriptive problem — that of stating English-specific rules for the identification of Subjects and Objects in simple verb-medial active sentences. Such a task is easily accomplished via the following two C-rules:

(1)　OBJECT RULE (OR)
An NP to the right of a nonpassive predicate P is analyzable as OBJ(P).

(2)　SUBJECT RULE (SR)
An NP to the left of a nonpassive predicate P is analyzable as SUBJ(P).

Note that the two rules make reference to the relations 'to the right/ left of', and not to the more restrictive 'to the IMMEDIATE right/left of'. Thus the possibility of an argument of P being indefinitely far from P in either direction is allowed for. On the other hand, it is also clear that not every NP to the right of a given predicate in a sentence can be OBJ(P), nor can every NP to the left of a predicate be SUBJ(P). For example, in the coordinate sentence

(3)　Harry kissed Maxine and Fred hugged Samantha.

only *Maxine* is OBJ*(kiss)*, and only *Fred* is SUBJ*(hug)*. Thus, the rules must be constrained in such a way as to prevent marking *Fred* or *Samantha* as OBJ*(kiss)* or *Harry* or *Maxine* as SUBJ*(hug)*; this problem receives extensive attention in Chapters 3-5. For the moment we will set the problem aside, focusing on other properties of the rules under discussion.

A pair of rules such as the OR and SR as stated in (1)-(2) can be made to work, but there is little inherent interest in them as they stand. They are *ad hoc* and will, moreover, not suffice to handle all cases. For example, there are intransitive sentences in which the Subject occurs to the right of the predicate — e.g.,

(4)   a. In walked Harry.
       b. There came a man.
       c. Away went Fred.

for which it would appear that the rules must be complicated with an attendant increase in the *ad hoc* character of the entire system. This is only an appearance, however; while it is not possible to completely eliminate *ad hoc* rules such as those in (1-2), we can eliminate some. In particular, we can eliminate the SR and avoid requiring a Subject identification rule for sentences like those in (4). We accomplish this by introducing a system of metaconditions, accompanied by certain suppositions concerning their interaction with C-rules.

2.2. Metaconditions: A Proposed System and Its Consequences

2.2.1. *Statement of the Metaconditions*

As defined in the previous chapter, metaconditions are universal constraints which, taken together, jointly define the notion 'possible corepresentation' by virtue of defining what can be a possible predication for any natural language. By incorporating such constraints into grammatical theory, we accomplish two purposes: we provide a specific hypothesis concerning intrinsic limitations of possible languages, and we simplify the grammars of particular languages. The metaconditions to be assumed here are as follows:

(5)   LAW OF CORRESPONDENCE
       To every nonexpletive nonvocative NP in a sentence, there
       must correspond a statement in relational representation
       identifying this NP as an argument of some predicate in a
       specified relation or marking the NP as the Object of a
       preposition or both.[1]

(6)   LAW OF UNIQUENESS
       a. No single element in a sentence may be analyzed as bearing
           more than one predicate-argument relation to a predicate,
           unless the conditions exist for the predicate to be interpreted
           reflexively.
       b. No two elements in a sentence may be analyzed as bearing
           the same predicate-argument relation to a single predicate,
           unless they are either coordinate or coreferential.

(7)   LAW OF ASSOCIATION
      An argument in the relation SUBJ must be associated with
      every predicate.[2]

2.2.2. *Interaction of Metaconditions and C-Rules*

Before examining and interpreting the metaconditions in detail, let us
show how they relate to the OR and SR. Suppose the OR is applied
to *Harry likes vodka;* the result is shown diagrammatically as follows:

(8)   HARRY   LIKE   VODKA
                                          OBJ

Notice that *Harry* can now be identified as SUBJ*(like)* without the SR,
since only its identification as such will permit all metaconditions to be
satisfied. By Correspondence, *Harry* must be an argument of *like* in some
relation; moreover, by Association, *like* must have a Subject. But this is
exactly the result obtained if the complete analysis is given as

(9)   HARRY   LIKE   VODKA
                    SUBJ   OBJ

In other words, *Harry*'s status can be DEDUCED if we know that *vodka*
is the Object; given the metaconditions, we may identify Subjects 'by
default', and no *ad hoc* C-rule such as the SR need be given.[3] In the case
of sentences such as those in (4), only one nonexpletive NP appears in
each case, and the predicates are intransitive, which is to say that they
do not take Objects. Thus the |non expletive NP can, given the Law of
Association, only be the Subject in each case. (Of course, these NPs
could also be marked as Objects by the OR, since they occur to the
right of the predicates. But the OR says only that an NP to the right of
a predicate is ANALYZABLE as the Object of that predicate, not that
it MUST be so analyzed. The precise significance of the locution
'analyzable as' will be dealt with in §2.2.4.)

2.2.3. *Further Commentary on the Metaconditions*

We must now submit the metaconditions themselves to careful examination. The first of these, the Law of Correspondence, has the formal

function of defining the conditions under which an analysis is complete or, more accurately, of defining the NECESSARY conditions for completeness. In other words, if this metacondition has not been satisfied, then the relational structure of the sentence under analysis cannot yet be considered to have been fully specified. If for any reason it should turn out to be impossible to satisfy the Law of Correspondence, the sentence under analysis is predicted to be anomalous in a particularly fundamental way. We will see later that the ill-formedness of sentences which, in transformational terms, violate the Complex NP and Coordinate Structure Constraints is due to the fact that they cannot be analyzed in such a way as to satisfy Correspondence.

The Law of Uniqueness is in two parts, each of which imposes a particular restriction on analyses but with a specific mitigating condition in each case. One role of this metacondition is complementary to that of the Law of Correspondence: whereas Correspondence is concerned with determining when an analysis can stop, Uniqueness guarantees that it WILL stop after it has been completed. If no such guarantee were provided, then there would be no principled reason to take (9) as the complete analysis of *Harry likes vodka;* one could, for example, continue the analysis to obtain

(10)

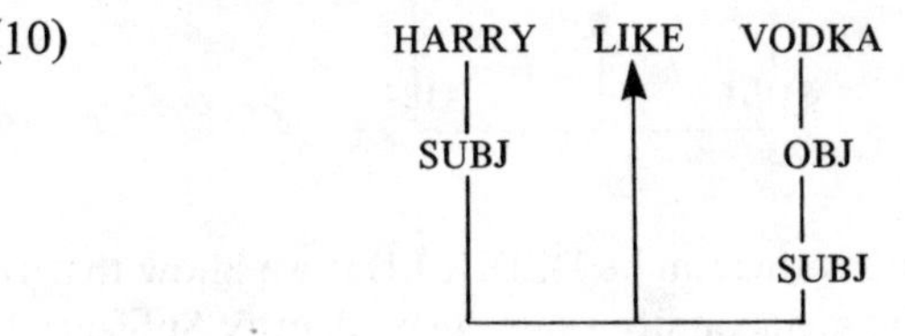

This analysis violates neither Correspondence nor Association, and yet it is incorrect. But (10) violates both Uniqueness-a (since *vodka* is in two relations with *like,* though *like* does not have a reflexive interpretation in this sentence) and Uniqueness-b (because *like* is analyzed as having two Subjects, whereas the NPs so analyzed are neither coreferential nor coordinate). As examples of situations in which the mitigating conditions would apply, consider

(11)   a. Harry likes himself.
       b. Harry shaved.
       c. Harry and George like vodka

The analysis of (11a) proceeds as follows: First, by the OR, we determine that *himself* = OBJ*(like)*. By a general principle, we regard any predicate having a reflexive pronoun as Object as being reflexive — i.e., as entering into a predication in which Subject and Object are presumed identical; by a second general principle, we regard any reflexive pronoun marked as OBJ(P) as necessarily coreferential with SUBJ(P). Once *Harry* is identified as SUBJ*(like)*, the following analysis may be obtained:

(12)

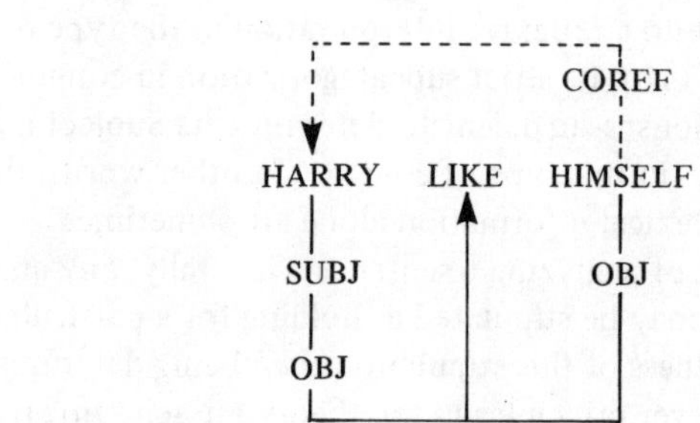

At this point, a further condition comes into play:

(13) TRANSMISSION PRINCIPLE
　　　　A nonanaphoric NP serving as antecedent to a pronoun marked
　　　　a(P) must itself be analyzed as a(P).

where a is some predicate-argument relation. The antecedent of a pronoun is defined formally as a nonanaphoric NP with which the pronoun is marked coreferential; thus, an anaphoric pronoun 'transmits' its relational status to its antecedent, the result in this case leading to the final analysis

(14)

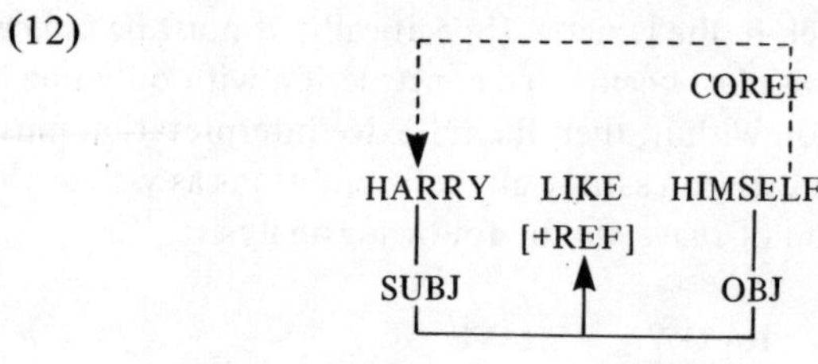

We thus see that in (11a) *Harry* designates both the individual 'doing the liking' and the individual liked, consistent with the definition of 'reflexively interpreted predicate'. It is to make such analyses as (14) possible that this specific mitigating condition is written into

Uniqueness-a.

A quite different kind of case is represented by (11b). In analyzing this sentence, we face the following situation: *shave* is transitive and thus requires an Object, but there is no NP to its right, and hence the OR is inapplicable. However, *shave* is one of a class of verbs which are subject to a reflexive interpretation in just such constructions as (11b); the members of this class (including *wash* and *dress* as well as *shave*) must be marked as such in the lexicon. (Specifically, it must be indicated that if a member of this class occurs in a construction with only one NP analyzable as in relation with it, then the reflexive interpretation must be imposed.) Note that we can satisfy all metaconditions as well as the strict subcategorization of *shave* via the following analysis:

(15)

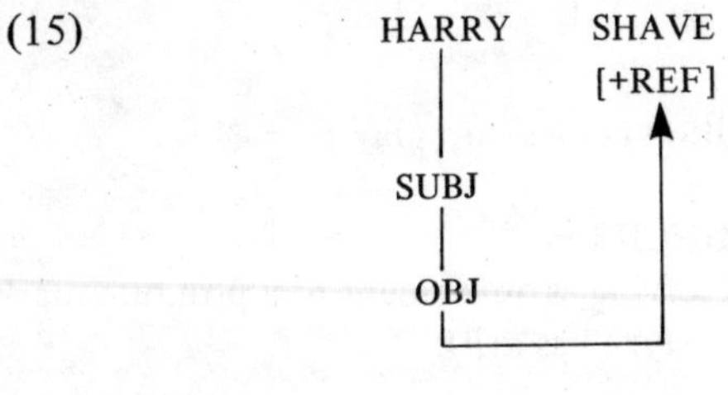

This case is important, since it illustrates a fundamental assumption underlying corepresentational analysis — namely, that even though C-rules are sometimes needed to identify arguments with a specified function, they are not always needed to identify such arguments. Although Objects must be identified by C-rule in some cases, they need not be so identified in all. As long as *shave* is marked in the lexicon as susceptible to a reflexive interpretation in the type of context involved in (11b), its strict subcategorization in conjunction with the metaconditions is sufficient to determine its Subject and Object when it occurs in this type of context. In other words, the metaconditions and lexical information alone are sometimes sufficient to the task of analyzing a sentence. Generally, any analysis (or subpart thereof) may be stipulated as holding for a particular sentence, the correctness of this stipulation then being determined on the basis of whatever principles in the theory are reievant. If no principle is violated by the stipulation, then it is presumed valid, and the ensuing analysis is permitted to stand. Put even more succinctly, whatever analysis 'works', given the theory, is permissible, regardless of how it was obtained.

The third mitigating condition on Uniqueness involves coordinate

NPs, as in (11c). In this case *Harry* and *George* must both be marked as SUBJ*(like)*, which is possible for conjoined NPs given the formulation of Uniqueness-b. We are assuming, of course, that the conditions under which two NPs may be presumed coordinate may be formally defined; this matter is taken up in detail in Chapter 5.

The Laws of Uniqueness and Correspondence are jointly involved in the characterization of the ill-formedness of a particular type of deviant sentence, e.g.,

(16)   *Who did Harry kiss the girl?

Since *kiss* is two-place, its subcategorization can be satisfied by selection as arguments of any of the three pairs of NPs *(who, Harry), (Harry, the girl),* or *(who, the girl);* whichever pair is chosen, there will be an NP left over. This NP cannot be left unanalyzed, since Correspondence would then be violated; but it cannot be analyzed as either Subject or Object of *kiss* since there would then be either two Subjects or two Objects that are neither coreferential nor coordinate, in violation of Uniqueness-b. The sentence is thus 'overloaded', to use terminology that will be adopted in Chapter 4.

As a final observation concerning the Law of Uniqueness, let us note that as stated it imposes no prohibition on a single NP being analyzed as an argument of more than one predicate. Moreover, it is clear that such a prohibition would be incorrect, since it would predict inadmissibility for sentences such as

(17)   a. Harry wants to drink vodka.
       b. Harry wants to be kissed by Maxine.

for which the correct analyses may be given (in part) as

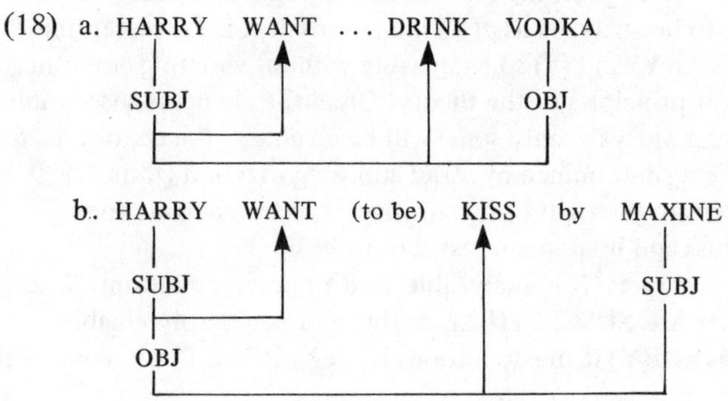

The last of the metaconditions, the Law of Association, must not be misunderstood. Though it requires that every predicate be analyzed as having a Subject (i.e., that a specification of its Subject be given in the relational representation of the sentence in which it occurs), it does NOT require that the Subject occur overtly in the surface sentence. The means by which null Subjects are recovered will be taken up in §2.3.

2.2.4. *On the Interpretation of C-Rules*

We now take up the matter of giving a precise interpretation to 'is analyzable as' as this expression is employed in the OR. To say that X is analyzable as $a(Y)$ does not mean that it must be analyzed as $a(Y)$; example (3), for instance, has three NPs to the right of the verb *kiss,* only one of which can actually be analyzed as OBJ*(kiss)*. On the other hand, analyzability cannot be interpreted so weakly as to permit analyses like

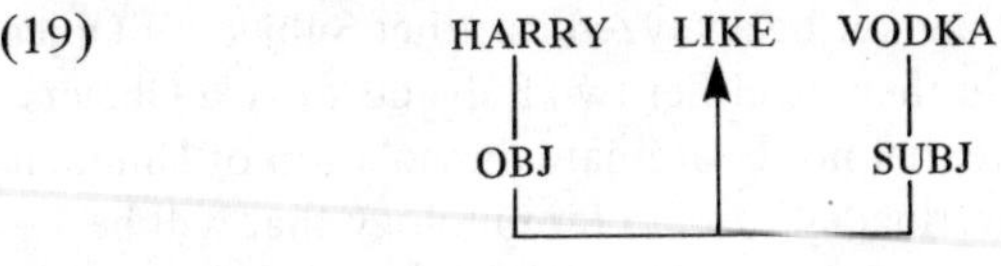

If 'X is analyzable as $a(Y)$ under conditions K' is taken to mean only that the conditions K constitute a situation in which the OPTION exists to analyze X as $a(Y)$, then (19) ought to be perfectly possible. The reason is that it satisfies all metaconditions; it cannot, moreover, be taken as violating the OR if that rule is given the weakest possible interpretation.

To resolve this difficulty, we must make the following distinction: We will say that an element is SUSCEPTIBLE to analysis as $a(Y)$ if the conditions for its being so analyzed by some C-rule are met; so, for example, all NPs to the right of a verb are susceptible to analysis as Object of the verb, given the OR. We will say that an element is ELIGIBLE to be analyzed as $a(Y)$ if and only if it is (a) susceptible to analysis as $a(Y)$ and (b) so analyzable without violating any other conditions or principles of the theory. Of all the elements susceptible to a particular analysis, only some will be eligible — the conditions for eligibility being determined by strict subcategorization (thus rendering NPs to the right of intransitive verbs as ineligible for Object status) and by domain restrictions.

We now interpret 'X is analyzable as $a(Y)$ under conditions K' as meaning that X is SUSCEPTIBLE to (but not necessarily eligible for) analysis as $a(Y)$ if the conditions K are satisfied. But in conjunction with this interpretation, we impose the following crucial constraint:

(20) FIRST MAXIMIZATION PRINCIPLE[4]
 If X is eligible to be analyzed as OBJ(Y) by the OR,
 it must be so analyzed.

Given the First Maximization Principle, analysis (19) can be ruled out. Since *vodka* is eligible to be analyzed as OBJ*(like)*, the constraint says that it must be so analyzed. In the case of the coordinate sentence (3), domain restrictions will restrict the verb *kiss* to being able to take as arguments only elements within its own conjunct; consequently, *Maxine* is the only NP in that sentence eligible for analysis as OBJ*(kiss)*.

2.2.5. *On the Status of Subjects*

The *modus operandi* that we have adopted for Subject and Object identification is such that Objects are identified by C-rule (the OR) and Subjects are identified deductively on the basis of the results of applying the OR and the restrictions imposed by the metaconditions — thus enabling us to eliminate the SR. As it happens, however, it would have been equally possible to eliminate the OR, keep the SR, and identify Objects deductively. For example, suppose we applied the SR to obtain

(21) 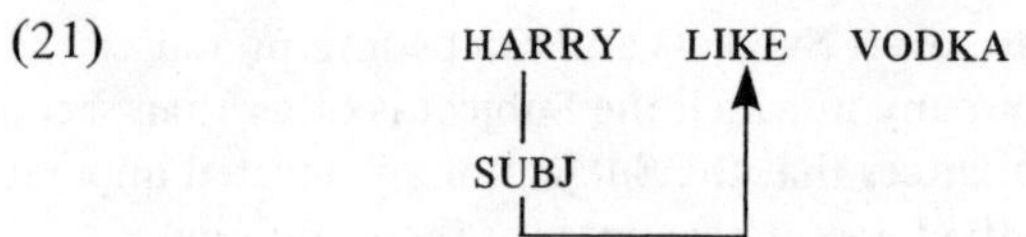

That *vodka* must be OBJ*(like)* will then follow, since (a) this NP cannot be left unanalyzed; (b) *like* requires an Object, and (c) the requirements in (a) and (b) can both be satisfied only if *vodka* is so analyzed. Consequently, all that can really be shown at this point is that EITHER the OR or the SR can be eliminated; we have as yet no clear grounds for preferring one approach over the other. Notice also that even though the SR as given above applies only to the case where the Subject precedes its predicate, the rule need not be complicated for cases where the Subject follows an intransitive verb, since they may be handled without recourse to C-rules.

There are two comments to be made on this situation:

(a) We will see presently (§2.4) that even without the SR, there are some cases where Subject identification must be accomplished by

C-rule; our assumption that Subjects are identified deductively, if correct, is valid only insofar as active sentences are concerned. In passives, the situation reverses itself.

(b) None the less, the validity of our assumption for the active case can be defended on the grounds that it allows certain facts to be explained. In Chapter 3, it will be shown that certain differences in the behavior of Subject and Object complements are a natural consequence of this assumption; an analogous argument is given in Chapter 4 with regard to the behavior of complex NPs.

For the moment, we will operate in a manner consistent with the claim that there is an OR but no SR, recognizing that justification for doing so has yet to be established.

2.3. Null Constituents

We now take up the matter of recovering arguments of predicates with null surface realization. The principles required are of varying degrees of generality. One quite general principle applies to imperatives and may be stated thus:

(22) IMPERATIVE SUBJECT CONDITION
For any V interpreted as imperative, ADDRESSEE = SUBJ(V).[5]

Applied to English, this principle serves two functions: It limits the class of sentences which have overt Subjects and can be interpreted as imperative by ruling out any in which the Subject is other than second person; but it also guarantees that the Subject of a truncated imperative will be correctly identified, i.e., it accounts for the traditional grammarian's 'understood *you*'. In terms of this principle, we can also explain the facts exhibited in the well-known paradigm

(23) a. Wash yourself!
     b. *Wash himself!
     c. *Wash you!
     d. *Wash him!

In (23a) *yourself* is analyzed as OBJ*(wash)* by the OR, and this in turn imposes a reflexive interpretation on the verb; we thus determine that its Subject may also act as Object. By the Imperative Subject Condition, we ultimately obtain

(24)

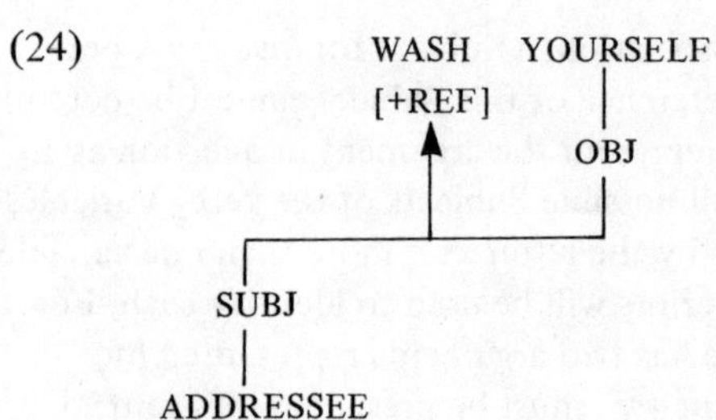

(Recovered arguments will always be placed below the line linking them to their associated predicates.) But a reflexive Object must be coreferential with the Subject of its predicate; after transmission, the final analysis emerges as

(25)

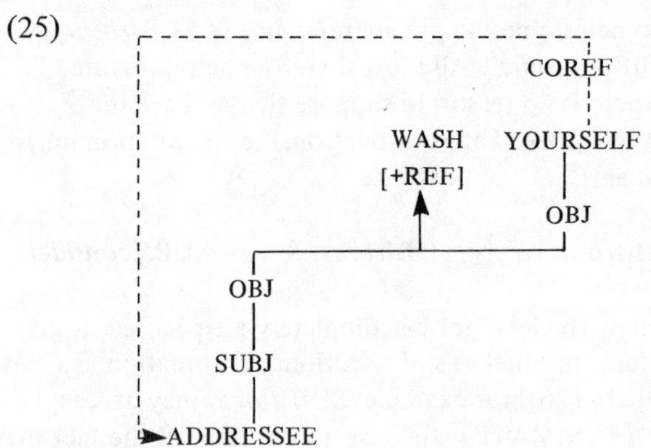

In (23b), by contrast, there is a conflict: Since the Object is in the third person, it cannot be coreferential with the Subject (since a third person pronoun can never have the addressee as referent); but this then violates the requirement that a reflexive Object be coreferential with the Subject of its predicate. In (23d), however, this problem does not arise, since the Object, while third person, is not reflexive. Finally, in (23c) Subject and Object must be presumed coreferential, since both refer to the addressee; but the sentence then violates the rule of English requiring that the Object of a predicate take reflexive form if coreferential with the Subject.

Consider now the case of truncated passives, e.g.,

(26) Harry was loved.

According to the Law of Association, a Subject for *love* must be identified, but the precise reference of this Subject cannot be determined. In such a circumstance, we represent the argument in question as a variable which ranges over all possible Subjects of the verb. Variables will be indicated generically by the letter x; if more than one variable enters into an analysis, subscripts will be used to identify each. For example, if a single sentence has two arguments represented by variables but the ranges of the two must be presumed different, the variables will be subscripted as x_1 and x_2. (More accurately, if the reference of two variable arguments must be presumed different, the variables will be distinguished by subscripts.) To cite one concrete instance, in

(27)   Being beaten is considered unhealthy.

there is no way to determine the precise reference of SUBJ*(beat)*, OBJ*(beat)*, or SUBJ*(consider)*. All must therefore be represented as variables, but there is no reason to suppose that all have the same (stipulated) reference. Thus our relational representation might include the statements

(28) x_1 = SUBJ*(beat)* & x_2 = OBJ*(beat)* & x_3 = SUBJ*(consider)*

A variable may, none the less, not be completely unspecified; it may acquire some features on the basis of selectional information associated with the predicate. In (26), for example, SUBJ*(love)* may at least be determined to be [+ANIMATE], thereby accounting for the fact that if a hearer should wish to request more information of a speaker who utters (26), he would inquire 'By whom?' but not '*By what?'

Truncated passives may be regarded as subject to the following principle:

(29)   TRUNCATED PASSIVE CONDITION
       If a predicate P occurs on the surface in passive form and
       SUBJ(P) does not occur overtly on the surface, enter a
       statement x_i = SUBJ(P) into the relational representation.

where i represents a possible subscript.

Highly idiosyncratic recoverability conditions are also required, as in cases like

(30)   Harry drinks.

Here the Object of *drink* can only be understood as designating the class of alcoholic beverages, an item of information that must be associated with this particular verb in the lexicon.

2.4. Passive Constructions

We now undertake a more detailed examination of sentences in passive form – e.g.,

(31) Vodka is liked by Harry.

To set matters in perspective, let us first compare (31) to

(32) *Vodka is liked Harry.

The ill-formedness of (32) may be accounted for via the following rule:

(33) PASSIVE SUBJECT RULE (PSR)
      If the Subject of a passive predicate occurs on the surface,
      it must be Object of the preposition *by*.

Setting aside, for the moment, the problem of specifying the conditions under which an NP is determined to be the Object of a preposition, let us consider the various tasks which the PSR can be made to perform. That we need such a rule in any event is shown by cases like (32); but there are various attractive spinoff results as well. Consider a truncated passive such as

(34) Harry is loved.

for which the correct analysis is

(35)

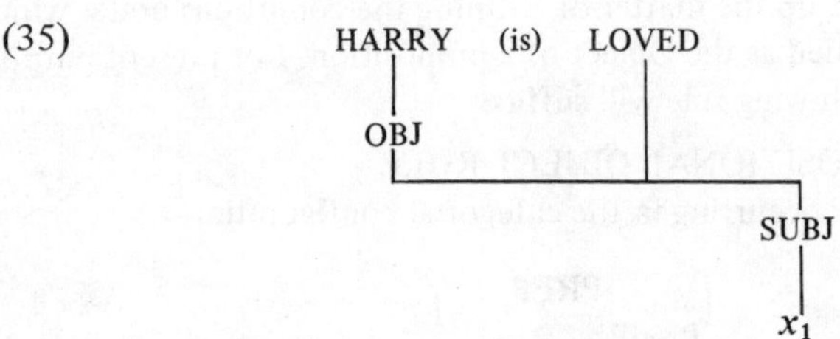

In order to know that this sentence must be analyzed as having a variable in the role of Subject, we must know that this argument does not appear on the surface; that is, we must know in advance that

Harry is not SUBJ*(love)*. Given the PSR, this vital information can be readily obtained. Moreover, given the PSR, we need no special rules for Object identification in passives — a consequence that is desirable, since in truncated passive constructions there is no fixed position for Objects, as shown by

(36) a. Many martyrs are buried here.
     b. Here are buried many martyrs.

That is, if we did seek to identify passive Objects via rules referring to relative order of elements (as we have proposed for active Objects), two such rules would be necessary; but the necessity for any such rules can be avoided given the PSR. We can, in other words, implement a treatment in which passive Objects are identified deductively.

The PSR can thus be taken as fulfilling the same function for passive sentences as the OR fulfils for active sentences (though this is not the PSRs only function, since its primary motivation was to enable us to rule out sentences like (32)). It is characterizable, in other words, as a C-rule according to the definition in §1.2: applied to a sentence like (31) the PSR identifies the relational status of *Harry* on the basis of some other item of information (i.e., that this NP is OBJ(*by*). (In general, C-rules are defined in terms of content and function, rather than form; thus, the fact that the PSR is not of precisely the same form as the OR is of no consequence with regard to its status as a C-rule.)

If we are correct in our approach to active sentences, then actives and passives are inverses of each other in the sense that arguments identified by C-rule in one are identified deductively in the other and vice versa. We will make use of this inverse relationship presently in defining what we will call 'argument markedness'.

We now take up the matter of defining the conditions under which an NP is identified as the Object of a preposition. For present purposes at least, the following rule will suffice:

(37) PREPOSITIONAL OBJECT RULE
     An NP occurring in the categorial configuration

$$[_{\text{PrepP}} \quad \text{PREP} \quad \underline{\quad\quad} \quad]$$

must be analyzed as OBJ(PREP); if a preposition fails to occur with any NP as a sister, its Object must be the leftmost eligible NP.

The latter part of the rule accounts for sentences with stranded prepositions such as

(38) Fred, vodka is liked by.

In our treatment of passives, Subject and Object are treated in the same way as Object and Subject respectively in actives. We will make formal recognition of this analogy in the following way: Henceforth, we will refer to active Objects and passive Subjects generically as MARKED arguments; by the same token, we will call active Subjects and passive Objects UNMARKED arguments. (Henceforth, the notations u-ARG(P) and m-ARG(P) will be used to designate unmarked and marked arguments of P respectively.) The terminology alludes to the fact that what we are now calling marked arguments are identified via special rules making reference to specific structural cues, at least in constructions of the type now under discussion, whereas no such special rules are needed in the unmarked case. The verbiage here, however, should not be taken overly seriously; the labels 'marked' and 'unmarked' are primarily a matter of convenience.

2.5. Oblique Distance

We conclude this chapter by examining constructions in which the verb follows its arguments — e.g.,

(39) Vodka, Fred likes.

Here our new notion of argument markedness will be highly relevant. We begin by observing that in such constructions, the Object always precedes the Subject if the verb is in active form; the following examples illustrate (the Object is always in square brackets and the Subject in parentheses):

(40) a. [What] does (Harry) like?
      b. [The girl] that (Harry) likes.
      c. It's [vodka] that (Harry) likes.
      d. [Vodka] is what (Harry) likes.

(And, of course, (39) conforms to this pattern as well.) As a preliminary statement of this generalization, we may posit the following:

(41) If Subject and Object of an active predicate both precede the predicate, the Object must precede the Subject.

This will be sufficient to handle the sentences in (39-40). Now consider the following two passive sentences:

(42) a. It's by Harry that vodka is liked.
      b. *It's vodka that by Harry is liked.

Sentence (42b) seems noticeably worse than (42a), hence the asterisk; in other words, if in a passive sentence Subject and Object precede the predicate, it is evidently the Subject which must come first. We may account both for this fact and for (39-40) if we amend (41) to read as follows:

(43) OBLIQUE DISTANCE CONDITION (ODC)
      If u-ARG(P) and m-ARG(P) both precede P, it must be in the order m-ARG(P) $-u$-ARG(P).

That is, the marked argument must be farther from P than the unmarked argument — hence the use of 'distance' in the name of the rule.

The ODC, if taken as a rule of English grammar, serves two functions. Applied to passive sentences, it accounts for the preferability of sentences like (42a) to those like (42b); it is not needed to actually identify either argument as SUBJ or OBJ, since this can be done via the PSR, the metaconditions, and the strict subcategorization of *like*. Applied to an active sentence, however, the ODC does have an indirect argument-identifying function. Consider again (39): The OR will be inapplicable, since nothing occurs to the right of the predicate in this example; we therefore are forced to assume that OBJ(*like*) is to the left. But there are two NPs to the left of *like,* one of which is the Object, from which it follows that the other is the Subject. The ODC enables us to decide which is which; in principle, either of the following analyses is possible:

(44) a.

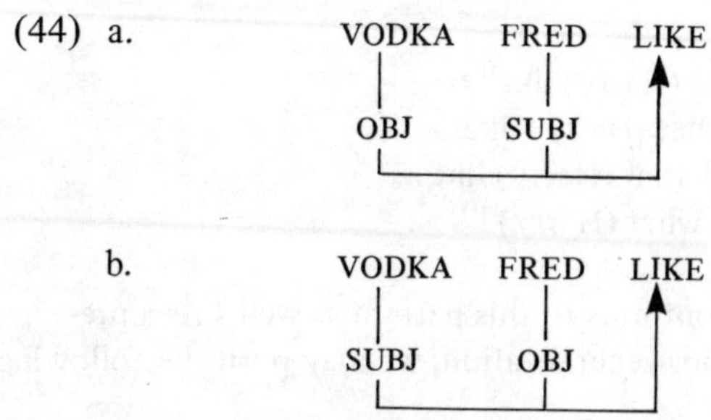

      b.

But according to the ODC, only (44a) is possible, since (a) the rule states that marked arguments must precede unmarked ones and (b) Objects are marked and Subjects unmarked in active constructions.

Since the ODC serves in the active case as a rule via which relational information may be recovered given a particular type of structural cue, and on a language-specific basis, it also has some of the earmarks of a C-rule. We will henceforth consider it one, which brings our inventory of such rules to four (counting the Prepositional Object Rule).

The ODC expresses a pervasive generalization with, as far as I can determine, only one class of exceptions. This involves constructions such as

(45)　a.

$$\text{The meat is} \begin{Bmatrix} \text{tough} \\ \text{ready} \\ \text{hot enough} \\ \text{too hot} \end{Bmatrix} \text{for Harry to eat.}$$

　　　b. (It's) for Harry (that) the meat is . . . to eat.

In (45a) the arguments of *eat (the meat* and *Harry)* are in the order OBJ-SUBJ, consistent with the ODC; but as (45b) shows, the order can be reversed without altering the interpretation.[6] Let us adopt the label 'T' (mnemonic for *tough*) as a rubric beneath which to subsume members of a class which includes the transformationalist's '*tough*-Movement' adjectives, as well as *ready* and compound adjectives in the forms *too*-A and A-*enough;* we may then revise the ODC slightly as follows:

(46)　OBLIQUE DISTANCE CONDITION — Revised Formulation
　　　If u-ARG(P) and m-ARG(P) both precede P, it must be in the order m-ARG — u-ARG, except where P is immediately subordinate to a T-predicate.

The crucial property which all T-predicates have in common is that they allow their own Subjects to act as Objects of their complements — as in (45a), where *the meat* is OBJ*(eat)*; this is not the case in comparable constructions with other predicates — e.g.,

(47)　George is eager for Harry to eat.

where *George* may bear no relation to *eat* whatsoever; it could only act as an argument of *eat* (as Subject) in a sentence such as

(48) George is eager to eat.

Thus, in a sentence like

(49) *George is eager (for Harry) to like.

we will have ungrammaticality, since *like,* unlike *eat*, requires an overt Object on the surface and no NP is available to be so analyzed in the sentence in question. In transformational terms, these facts would be accounted for by restricting Equi-NP Deletion in the 'normal' case to the deletion of subordinate Subjects (underlying or derived); other predicates require lexical marking permitting them to govern special movement or deletion rules resulting in the derivation of surface structures such as (45a).

Regardless of the theoretical model we adopt, T-predicates and their associated constructions are going to be problematical given the present state of our knowledge. I have, admittedly, no new insights to present here, my purpose being only to fix exactly the scope of the ODC; I will therefore not consider T-predicates further, though I do not wish to minimize the importance and interest of further study of their nature.

The ODC and the constructions to which it has been seen to pertain define one interesting point of comparison between CORG and TG. To account for the relevant facts, as exemplified in the paradigm (39-40) a transformational account of English would adduce a series of transformations each of which would have among its effects a structural change conforming to the schema

(50) $NP_1 \ldots P \ldots NP_2 \Longrightarrow NP_2 \ldots NP_1 \ldots P$

thus allowing such derivations as

(51) a. Harry likes vodka $\Longrightarrow$ Vodka, Harry likes.
$\qquad NP_1 \qquad\quad NP_2$

 b. George thinks Harry likes vodka $\Longrightarrow$
$\qquad\qquad\qquad NP_1 \qquad\quad NP_2$
Vodka, George thinks Harry likes.[7]

 c. George thinks Harry likes vodka. $\Longrightarrow$
$\qquad NP_2 \qquad\qquad NP_2$
Harry, George thinks likes vodka.[8]

In (51b, c) the input structure is the same in both cases; but whereas the subordinate clause Object is moved in the first case, the Subject of that clause is moved in the second. Evidently, then, this type of movement is 'functionally blind' — it is not sensitive to the argument role of the element being moved. Now consider the sentence

(52) Harry knows a girl that likes Fred.

If *Fred* were to be moved in accordance with schema (50), we would obtain

(53) *Fred, Harry knows a girl that likes.

This sentence is ill-formed, a fact normally accounted for in transformational models by the Complex NP Constraint; see Chapter 4 for further discussion of the basis for this type of unacceptability. In the context of the present discussion, we will ignore the fact that (53) is deviant in a particular way and consider how it would normally be interpreted if it were to actually occur. Sentences such as this are in fact interpretable with a little effort; an attempt at processing (53) will yield, despite the relative unacceptability of the sentence, an interpretation such that *Fred* is OBJ*(like)* and *a girl* SUBJ*(like)*.[9] Notice, however, that we could also derive (53) from

(54) Harry knows a girl that Fred likes.

where *Fred* occurs as SUBJ*(like)*. Given that the schema (50) is functionally blind, (53) ought therefore to be ambiguous as between interpretations corresponding to (52) and (54); but this is not the case, and the question is why. One might, of course, seek simply to dismiss the question out of hand, since (53) is ill-formed in any case and hence (by one line of reasoning) there is no need to inquire as to its semantic properties or seek an account of them. I will defend the propriety of employing interpretive data about ill-formed sentences later in the discussion; for the moment, let us simply proceed.

As things presently stand, our movement analysis of the data makes a wrong prediction about (53), i.e., that it should be ambiguous in a certain way. Let us now consider how matters would look in a corepresentational treatment. Here there are no movement operations; rather, structures of the input and output forms in (50) are related via a set of principles which correlate surface configurational information with relational interpretations. The relevant principles applied to one or the other of the structures will yield the information that $NP_1 = SUBJ(P)$

and NP_2 = OBJ(P) (for the active case). Returning to (53), let us assume that we already have a way of determining in advance that *Fred* and *a girl* are the arguments of *like*. (The associated principles are developed in the next two chapters.) We thus have the configuration

(55) Fred . . . a girl . . . like

According to the ODC, then, we must have the analysis

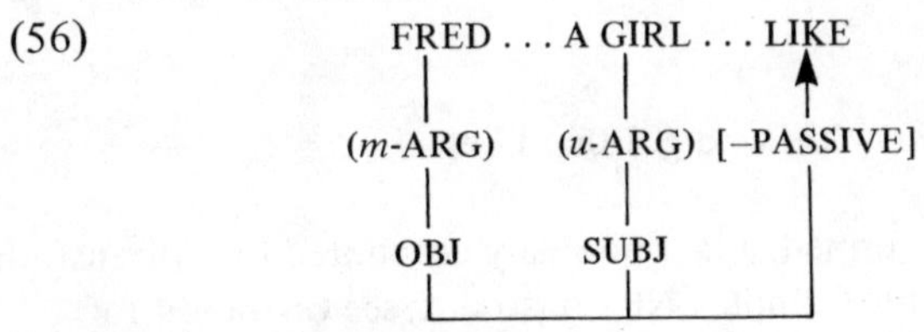

which is the correct result for the sentence in question; any other would violate the ODC. Now consider again the outputs of (51b, c) in relevant particulars:

(57) a. Vodka . . . Harry likes.
      b. Harry . . . likes vodka.

(*like* and arguments having been isolated, just as in (55)). The ODC is applicable only to (57a), since only in this sentence do the arguments of *like* precede; the analysis of (57b) can be accomplished via recourse to the OR and the metaconditions, just as any simple sentence of the form NP-V-NP, and the result will be that *Harry* is SUBJ*(like)* and *vodka* OBJ*(like)*. Whether the 'fronted' NP in constructions of this sort is a Subject or Object of its predicate depends on the relative configuration of NPs and predicate — there being two such configurations allowed, one consistent with a 'fronted' Object, the other with 'fronting' of the Subject. (My use of quotes here is intended to emphasize that 'fronting' of NPs as such is not recognized in CORG; the terminology is used solely for convenience.) In the case of (53), however, there is a single configuration parallel to (57a) and a single interpretation; the fact that this one configuration could in a transformational treatment be derived from two distinct underlying structures militates against such a treatment, given that the output structure is not actually ambiguous. On the other hand, the CORG approach, which deals directly with output, makes exactly the correct predictions.

In §1.7, we alluded to the 'relating function' of transformations. Transformations instantiating the movement schema (50) serve this function in that they establish a relational equivalence between structures of the forms cited: under such an interpretation, conditions for relational interpretation need be given only for the input structures, since predicate-argument relations remain invariant under transformation. But we have just seen a failure of transformations to fulfil the relating function adequately, whereas an alternative non-transformational approach does not fail in the same way. We noted that one of the advantages of TG was supposed to be that it provided a mechanism which simultaneously fulfilled the relating and surface structure generating functions for a large class of constructions; there may now be reasons to question whether this advantage actually exists.

I return now to an anticipated objection to the entire line of argument, namely, that deviant sentences like (53) are not properly used as a source of evidence. In reply, I begin by noting that test conditions for hypotheses typically require a certain amount of artifice. For example, direct observation of nature by physicists, chemists, or biologists must frequently be replaced by observation of a 'substitute nature' created in the laboratory and embodying conditions that may never obtain in nature itself. The experimental method in natural sciences derives its value from the fact that although the 'real world' is frequently too complex in some ways and too impoverished in others for naturalistic observation to be an adequate source of relevant data, a given hypothesis has consequences for the laboratory as well; if we were to dismiss all hypotheses given justification in the laboratory just because of the inherent artificiality of experimental situations, we would thereby dismiss science as we know it. The situation confronting us here is, in my view, no different. The crucial point is that ANY predictions made by an hypothesis are fair game in theory validation — even those that can only be tested in artificial situations; thus, if a linguistic hypothesis makes predictions about how speakers of a language will interpret certain structures, whether or not the structures are well-formed (or 'in the language') is quite beside the point — unless, of course, it could be demonstrated that speakers are not reliable in interpreting deviant utterances (a claim for which there is at present no evidence). I submit, then, that my methodology is entirely valid, even given the touch of artifice that it requires.

In this final section of the chapter, we have had to deal with complex sentences as well as with simplex ones and have had to take for granted the existence of a set of principles for isolating arguments of a given predicate in such sentences — what we labeled 'domain restrictions' in Chapter 1. The time has now come to attack the domain problem directly; it is with regard to the syntax of complex sentences that the theory is subjected to the true acid test.

Notes

1. By 'expletive' NP we mean items such as *there* in (4b) or *it* in sentences like *It annoyed me that the butter was rancid.*
2. A problem is posed, of course, by 'Subjectless' sentences such as *It rained.* Conceivably, the Law of Association should be narrowed to refer to predicates of at least one place; on the other hand, if *rain* and similar verbs are treated as 'zero-place predicates' one might well ask whether they are predicates at all. And, of course, the possibility must not be discounted that such verbs might yet be found to take Subjects of some as yet undetermined kind.
3. It is possible in principle to proceed in exactly reverse fashion, i.e., to identify Subjects by C-rule and Objects by deduction. See §2.2.5 for discussion.
4. A 'Second Maximization Principle' interacting with this constraint will be given in Chapter 3. The rationale for the use of the term 'maximization' will become apparent at that point.
5. The conditions under which a verb may be construed as imperative must, of course, be stated. In English the requirement is that the verb (or its associated auxiliary, if there is one) appear in uninflected form.
6. The significance of these examples was pointed out to me by Anne Utschig.
7. The schema may also be instantiated, with the same result, by

$$\underset{\text{NP}_1}{\text{George thinks Harry likes vodka}} \implies \underset{\text{NP}_2}{\text{Vodka, \ldots}}$$

8. The output structure here may be somewhat awkward for some speakers; as an alternative, consider *Who does George think likes vodka?*, which can be given an analogous derivation.
9. This point has been checked with informants, who are unanimous on the point of interpretation in question.

3   COMPLEX SENTENCES I: COMPLEMENTATION

3.1. Background

3.1.1. *Some Definitions*

We define a COMPLEMENT as a predication which acts as an argument of a predicate. A predication Pr/P_i is SUBORDINATE to a predication Pr/P_j iff Pr/P_i is included, properly or otherwise, is an argument of P_j (This is a conception of subordination that is somewhat different from the standard one; see below.) We may illustrate with the sentences

(1)   a. Harry knows that Fred likes vodka.
       b. Harry knows that George believes that Fred likes vodka.

whose analyses may be given respectively as

(2)   a.

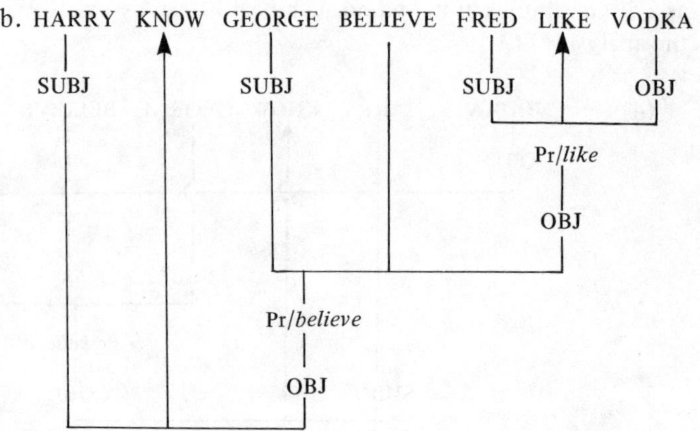

b.

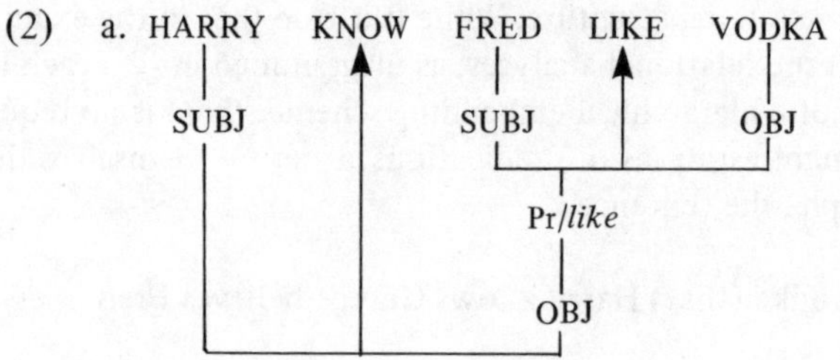

According to these analyses, *know* in each case has an Object in the form of a predication. In (2a) Pr/*like* is analyzed as OBJ*(know)* and is thus subordinate to Pr/*know*; we may say that it is IMMEDIATELY subordinate to Pr/*know*, since it is not properly included in any other predication itself subordinate to Pr/*know*. In (2b), however, Pr/*like* is not immediately subordinate to *know*, since it is properly included in Pr/*believe* — which IS immediately subordinate to Pr/*know*. Although we have defined subordination as a relation among predications, we will find it convenient to use the notion informally in such a way as to impute relations of subordination to other elements as well. Thus, in a structure like (2b) we might say that *Fred* is subordinate to *George* on the basis of the subordination relation between the predications containing these two NPs; or that *like* is subordinate to *know*, on the same grounds. The MAIN predicate of a sentence is that predicate which is not subordinate to any other — i.e., not a member of any subordinate predication.

As defined here, the relation 'subordinate to' is not equivalent to 'embedded in'. While these locutions are commonly used interchangeably, they will not be so used in this study. Embedding is a notion relevant to categorial representation, whereas subordination as we have defined it is associated with relational structure. While it is true that in the example sentences of (1) the relational analyses, as diagrammed in (2), each have the appearance of a hierarchical embedding scheme, there is no requirement that the manifestations of predications structure themselves this way. For example, the sentence

(3)   (It's) vodka (that) Harry knows George believes Fred likes.

has the same predicational structure as (1b); but now Pr/*like* is manifested as a discontinuous unit, and no such neat hierarchy exists. We may diagram the analysis of (3) as

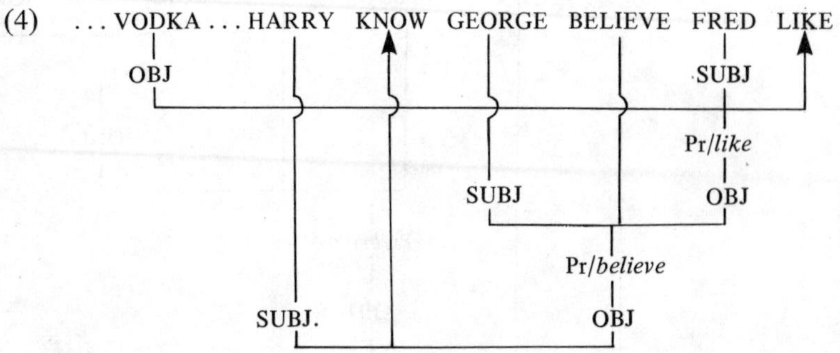

It is important to distinguish between a PREDICATION and a PRE-DICATION MANIFESTATION (or 'PRM'). A predication is a unit whose membership is determined on the basis of relational structure, since it is in relational representation that arguments are associated with predicates. A PRM is a unit in categorial structure, defined as consisting of the elements of some predication in some geometric configuration. In (1b) the PRM of Pr/*like* is the sequence *Fred likes vodka*; in (3) the PRM of this same predication is *Vodka . . . Fred likes.*

A sentence is in NORMAL FORM iff all PRMs in the sentence are continuous. Accordingly, (1a, b) are both in normal form, but (3) is not. The fact that complement constructions are not confined to normal form is one of the most significant facts about the syntax of natural languages, and one that will be an important focus of attention in this chapter.

We conclude this discussion of essential properties of complement constructions with one further note about subordination — namely, that this relation is asymmetric: If Pr/P_i is subordinate to Pr/P_j then Pr/P_j is not subordinate to Pr/P_i. As we will see, this fact plays an important role in the implementation of a corepresentational theory of complementation.

3.1.2. *Problems to Be Considered*

All the main concerns of this chapter are related to a specific problem, the interest of which lies in the fact that its solution leads to natural answers to a number of significant questions. Consider again sentence (1a) and its analysis as shown in (2a). In order to obtain this analysis and to guarantee that it is the only one possible (as in fact it is), it is necessary to supplement the theory as outlined in the previous chapters with certain further conditions. Given what we have developed so far, there is no way to assure unique analyses for many unambiguous complex sentences. In the case of (1a), for example, we could satisfy all C-rules and metaconditions with the following spurious representation:

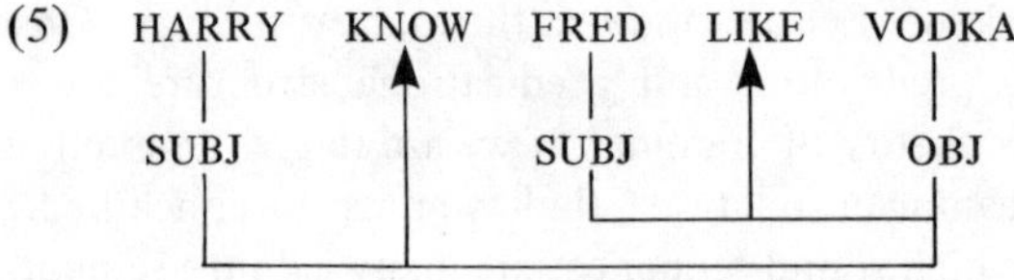

according to which (1a) ought to mean something like 'Harry knows vodka and Fred likes vodka'. Another possibility might be

(6)   HARRY   KNOW   FRED   LIKE   VODKA

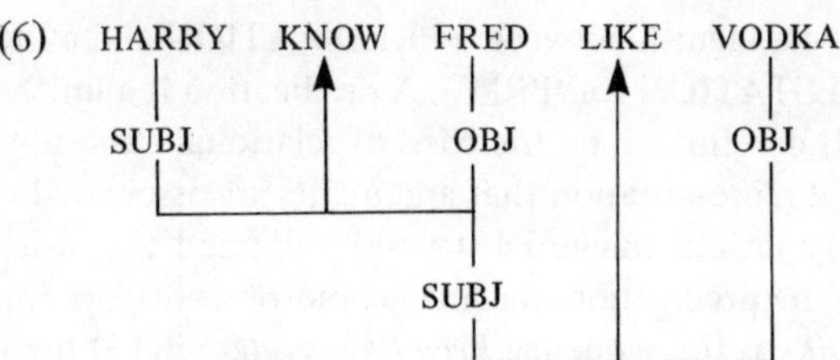

according to which the sentence ought to mean 'Harry knows Fred and Fred likes vodka'.[1]

The problem of limiting the range of possible analyses for complex sentences will be called the DOMAIN PROBLEM, where by the DOMAIN of a predicate P, we mean the portion of the sentence in which P occurs that is allowed to contain elements analyzable as arguments of P; the notation D/P will henceforth be used to designate the domain of P.

Our problem, in other words, is to determine for arbitrary complex sentences 'what goes with what' with regard to predicate-argument structure. The constraints that contribute to the solution of this problem are called DOMAIN RESTRICTIONS and constitute the third major component of a corepresentational grammar along with C-rules and meta-conditions. Whether or not the theory of domain restrictions to be developed here turns out to be universal remains to be seen; none the less, it will turn out to have considerable explanatory power with regard to the facts of English.

At this point I would like to anticipate and comment on a possible reaction from the transformational point of view to the foregoing discussion. A transformationalist critic of CORG might wish to argue that the notions 'domain restriction' and 'domain problem' are merely artefacts of the particular model and that the relevant issue has no significance if a transformational approach is adopted. Certainly there seems to be no clear recognition of the issue in the existing literature,[2] though I would claim that this is due to inattention rather than to the non-existence of the issue. Let us approach the matter this way: Observe first that the notions 'predication' and 'predicational structure' are relevant ones in ANY theory of grammar; if we are to give an explicit account of sound-meaning correlations, then we must be concerned with the manner in which sound sequences are analyzed into semantic units of various kinds, predications included. But the problem of identifying predications is precisely what we are here calling the domain problem. The classical transformational solution is to define an abstract categorial level, one of whose properties is that complement constructions always occur in normal form and maintain a particular type of hierarchical arrangement such that subordination relations are systematically reflected in embedding structure. Although transformationalists have rarely if ever been explicit on this score, it seems clear that they assume implicitly that D/P for any P is restricted to material commanded by P (symmetrically or asymmetrically) in the underlying P-marker of the sentence in which P occurs. (This is a necessary condition on the determination of D/P but not a sufficient one, as will be seen momentarily.) Suppose for example that (7) is an underlying P-marker associated with a sentence of some language:

(7)

$$S_0 \rightarrow NP_0 \quad V_0 \quad S_1 \rightarrow NP_1 \quad V_1$$

D/V_1, according to the implicit restriction, is confined to S_1 —and thus contains only NP_1. It never seems to be the case in transformational analyses that arguments of predicates are presumed to command their predicates asymmetrically. D/V_0 in (7) would — if I am correct in my interpretation of the TG model — include NP_0 and S_1 AS A WHOLE but no constituent of S_1. In other words S_1 is an argument of V_0 in (7), but NP_1 is not. If a particular nominal were to be simultaneously in two predications, it would have to be represented by different occurrences — as in

(8)

$$S_0 \rightarrow NP_0 \quad V_0 \quad NP_1^a \quad S_1 \rightarrow NP_1^b \quad V_1$$

Indeed, the contrast between P-markers such as (7) and (8) is commonly taken as the basis for distinguishing the predicational structures of sentences like

(9)   a. Harry expected Fred to go.
       b. Harry persuaded Fred to go.

If an advocate of TG were ever to give an explicit statement of the conditions for interpreting an underlying P-marker in terms of pre-dicational structure, the conditions required — whatever they turned out to be — would be domain restrictions in precisely our sense. The difference between TG and CORG is, therefore, not that one has to grapple with a domain problem while the other can avoid it; the difference pertains only to the kinds of structures on which domains are to be defined — surface structures (CORG) or hypothetical under-lying structures (TG).

Suppose our hypothetical critic concedes this point but now raises a second objection. Even granting that either theory must deal with the domain problem, the fact that surface structures can deviate from normal form means that their domain structure will be 'irregular'; therefore, he might argue, the transformational solution to the problem will be simpler and more general, since, by virtue of being defined only on underlying P-markers, domain restrictions in transformational theory need be given only for the normal form case. To put the matter in a different way, if more than one type of surface configuration can be a PRM, whereas only one type of underlying configuration can be, it would seem preferable to assume that domains are defined at the underlying level — in which case TG wins the day.[3]

Although this argument might seem persuasive at first, closer examination shows it to be fallacious. Our critic is forgetting something — namely, that if surface structure is irregular and underlying structure regular, then there is a discrepancy between the two that must be made up for somehow; the discrepancy is accounted for by a set of rules establishing correspondences between underlying P-markers and their surface reflexes, from which they may differ structurally in any of a variety of respects. So the issue really boils down to this: TG may be able to give simpler domain restrictions but at the cost of adding various *ad hoc* 'discrepancy rules' (transformations) to de-regularize the underlying structures; CORG may have to have more complicated domain restrictions, but it dispenses with the discrepancy rules. There is thus no basis for choice between the two on these grounds either .

In actuality a comparison between the corepresentational and transformational approaches on this score shows a much more interesting situation than a mere stalemate in which either compensates for its gains in one place by payment elsewhere. The kinds of deviation from normal form tolerated by natural languages appear to be quite severely constrained — a fact recognized by transformationalists, to be sure, in the context of the effort to 'limit the power' of transform-ations. The sum total of constraints on transformations may thus be taken as an expression of the precise degree to which the actual (surface structure) may differ from the ideal (underlying structure) and thus are of considerable interest. But this leads to a fundamental question: Should not the focus therefore be on the surface structures themselves (and limitations thereon) rather than on the rules which account for underlying-surface discrepancies? To see the force of this question, let us shift perspective and consider the domain problem from the CORG vantage point. In CORG we do not have the luxury of an idealized hypothetical categorial level; in defining domains, we must do so on actual surface structures, and in so doing we are therefore going to have to contend somehow with the fact that PRMs can take a variety of forms. Suppose, however, that we know (or at least believe) that the kind of variation found in surface domain structure is actually quite limited; such a belief would be well justified scientifically, since one generally prefers to assume that despite the apparent chaos that confronts our first unstructured observations, there is really an inherent order and systematicity in what we are observing. The following possibility then arises: Perhaps there is a single principle, or set of principles, which accounts both for normal form AND for observed instances of non-normal form; perhaps we can hit on just the right way of treating the former so that we can extend it without modification or alteration to the latter. Then one set of domain restrictions, defined on surface structure, would account for all possibilities. If such a result could be obtained, it would not only be aesthetically pleasing, it would have obvious explanatory interest. This would be so, since (a) if there is a well-motivated set of restrictions on the ideal structures and (b) it extends to the non-ideal cases, then the extent to which the latter may differ from the former is limited by these restrictions; and the constraints on deviation from the ideal are explained as due to the necessity for this deviation to extend no farther than what the few simple and independently motivated domain restrictions would allow. Let us now return to the original question, pertaining to whether the focus ought to be on rules or on structures. It seems reasonable to suppose that discrepancy rules (if we recognize them in syntactic theory) are constrained as they are because there are certain necessary limitations on what can be a possible surface structure or 'output'. But the question of WHY such limitations exist has either been ignored or presumed to be beyond 'pure' linguistics and left at the doorstep of the psychologists. I submit that at least some of the difficulties in finding satisfying explanations of linguistic phenomena are due not to

inherent limitations of autonomous linguistics but rather to the adoption
of a perspective within linguistics that wrongly orders the priorities. The
examination of output should, in my view, take centre stage, rather than
the formal study of rules.

I referred above to the interest of finding a set of well-motivated
domain restrictions for normal form that would also accommodate
actually existing deviations from normal form, and it is natural to ask
whether such a set can be found. I will present what I think is
convincing evidence in favor of an affirmative answer to this question.
Before proceeding, however, I wish to make a few further comments
in order to lay a foundation. Specifically, I wish to examine somewhat
more closely the reasoning which underlies the view that the existence
of non-normal form supports the transformational hypothesis. The
central argument runs as follows: If predications can be manifested
on the surface as discontinuous units, then not all PRMs are constituents
of surface structure; but if this is so, then surface constituent structure
fails to be indicative of an important feature of semantic organization.
Moreover, since the elements of a discontinuous PRM may be indefinitely
far apart, there is no one phrase structure configuration that can be
singled out as a PRM in non-normal form constructions. In normal form,
by contrast, every predication can be manifested as a constituent — i.e.,
as an S — and the interrelations among the predications can be determined
in a straightforward way in terms of the hierarchical relations among the
various S's of which the sentence is constituted. Moreover, the range of
configurations that can be construed as PRMs is limited to the range of
configurations analyzable as S's, given the phrase structure rules of the
grammar. Thus, the argument goes, predicational structure should be
defined only on normal form constructions, all non-normal form
constructions being derived therefrom via operations which by
definition preserve predicational structure but alter the manner in which
it is manifested.

One might, however, draw quite a different conclusion from the same
premise — namely, that S-node hierarchies are irrelevant to predicational
structure and that the existence of complement constructions in non-
normal form means only that some different system of surface
structure correlates is required if adequate conditions for determining
predicational structure are to be given. It is this latter conclusion that
will be argued for below; accordingly, we will assume that S-nodes do
not appear in categorial representation. The argument in support of this
conclusion will be divided into two parts: First, it will be shown that
it is POSSIBLE to construct a system of domain restrictions which does

not depend on S-node hierarchies; then it will be shown that such a system of restrictions is NECESSARY, since there are facts which are otherwise unexplained. The first part of the argument is presented in §§3.2.1-3.2.3 the second part in §3.2.4.

3.2. The Method

3.2.1. *Arguments and Argument Segments*

A predicational argument itself contains a predicate and its arguments. The elements of a predicational argument will be termed ARGUMENT SEGMENTS; formally, for any predicate-argument relation a and any predicate P, any NP, predicate, or predication which is included (properly or otherwise) in $a(P)$ is an a-segment with respect to P. So, for example, in (1a), *Fred, like,* and *vodka* are all Object segments with respect to *know*, as is Pr/*like*. (Every complete argument is a segment of itself.)

We now introduce the following conventions: Every predicate in a complex sentence is assigned a numerical index, the leftmost being indexed as '1', the next leftmost as '2', and so on. Let P be a predicate indexed as i; the notation as_i then denotes an a-segment with respect to P, i.e., with respect to the ith predicate in the sentence.

We noted above that every complete argument is a segment of itself; we will say that as_i is a MAXIMAL SEGMENT if it is coextensive with $a(P_i)$. For example, Pr/*like* in (2a) is a maximal Object segment with respect to *know*.

Nonpredicational arguments of predicates will be called ELEMEN-TARY arguments. It is important to note that there are predicates which may take either complements or elementary arguments in particular relations; for example, *know* may take predicational or elementary Objects, and *annoy* may take predicational or elementary Subjects:

(10) a. Harry knows that Fred likes vodka.
      b. Harry knows Fred.
(11) a. That Fred likes vodka annoys Harry.
      b. Fred annoys Harry.

Sentences involving such predicates will play an important part in the argumentation to be developed below.

The identification of elements as argument segments with respect to particular predicates will play an important role in the corepresentational treatment of complement constructions. The membership of PRMs of certain types is determined on the basis of argument segment identification, in a way to be described shortly. Before proceeding, however, we must modify two of our C-rules — the OR and the ODC — as follows:

(12) OBJECT RULE — Revised Formulation
An NP, predicate, or predication to the right of a nonpassive predicate P_i is analyzable as $OBJs_i$.

(13) OBLIQUE DISTANCE CONDITION — Revised Formulation
If u-$ARGs_i$ and m-$ARGs_i$ both precede P_i, it must be in the order m-$ARGs_i$ —u-$ARGs_i$, subject to exception cited in §2.5.

In other words, the two rules are reformulated so as to refer to argument segments rather than whole arguments — though they will none the less apply to whole arguments, since these are segments of themselves. In accordance with this reformulation, there is a slight change to be made in the First Maximization Principle:

(14) FIRST MAXIMIZATION PRINCIPLE — Revised Formulation
If X is eligible to be analyzed as $OBJs_i$ by the OR, it must be so analyzed.

In complex sentences, the OR will have numerous opportunites to apply; the First Maximization Principle guarantees that it will avail itself of as many of these opportunities as possible — thus making clear the reason for use of the term 'maximization'. The situation is somewhat different for the ODC, though this does not affect the validity of the principle as stated in (14).

We now define what we will call the STATUS of an argument segment: Let X be an element analyzed as an *as* with respect to predicates i through $i+n$; it will therefore bear indices i through $i+n$. Its status is simply this set of indices; that is, its status is an indication of which predicates, in the sentence in which X occurs, it is an a-segment with respect to. The notion of status figures crucially in the following domain restriction:

(15) SIMILARITY CONSTRAINT
If X and Y are both eligible to be analyzed as $a(P_i)$, then X always has priority of analyzability as $a(P_i)$ over Y if X is more similar in status to P_i than Y.

where similarity of status is defined formally as the number of indices that two as's have in common. In addition to this constraint, we also posit the following:

(16) ABSOLUTE PRIORITY CONSTRAINT
An NP identified as as_i has priority of analyzability as $a(P_i)$ over any NP not so identified.

The locution 'X has priority of analyzability as $a(P_i)$ over Y' means that Y cannot be considered a candidate for analysis as $a(P_i)$ until X has been accounted for. In other words, as a search is made for arguments of P_i, it must give preference to certain elements over certain others as candidates for inclusion in D/P_i.

In addition to the Absolute Priority and Similarity Constraints, we posit a further principle:

(17) SECOND MAXIMIZATION PRINCIPLE
A larger element has priority of analyzability as $a(P_i)$ over any smaller element so analyzable that it may contain, except where this would result in a predication being analyzed as an argument of its own predicate.

We have now laid the foundations for the development of a solution to the domain problem for sentences containing complements. The next two sections illustrate the manner in which the relevant principles apply.

3.2.2. *Marked Argument Complementation*

3.2.2.1. *Normal Form.* To illustrate the principles just introduced, we first apply them to the normal form Object complement construction (1b) — repeated here as

(18) Harry knows that George believes that Fred likes vodka.

Application of the OR in all possible instances yields

(19) HARRY KNOW GEORGE BELIEVE FRED LIKE VODKA

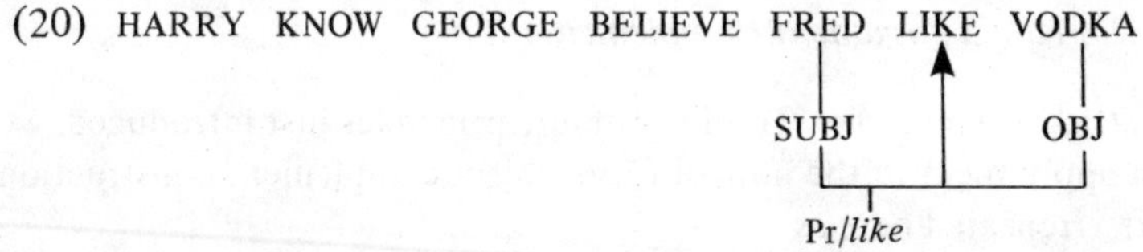

which by the First Maximization Principle must be assumed correct unless some violation ensues; that is, we are assuming that all elements to the right of P_i are eligible to be marked as $OBJs_i$, the correctness of this assumption being determined by the ability of the resulting analysis to satisfy all relevant principles of the theory without violation of any others. As it happens, the assumption in this case can be shown to be correct.

Observe now that *vodka* is identified as $OBJs_3$ and that no other NP is so identified; therefore, *vodka* is OBJ*(like)* by Absolute Priority. *Fred* must then be SUBJ*(like)*, since it is similar to *like* to degree 2, whereas *George* is similar to *like* only to degree 1, and *Harry* to degree 0, where 'similar to degree i' means 'having i indices in common with respect to the characterization *as*' (*a* in this case being OBJ). Thus the analysis at this point, in essential respects, may be given as

(20) HARRY KNOW GEORGE BELIEVE FRED LIKE VODKA

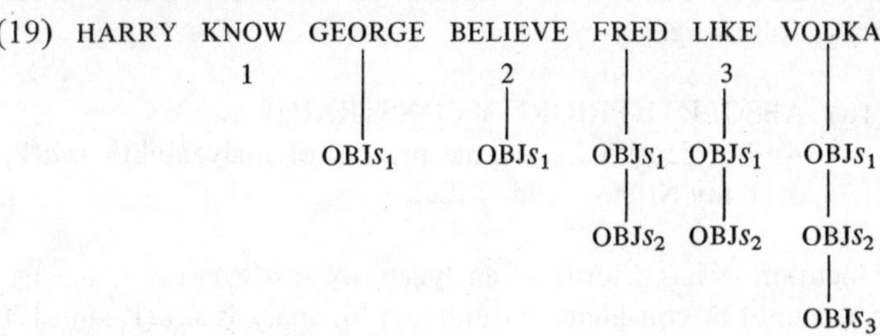

Given this much information, we may build up Pr/*believe* as follows: Both *Fred* and *vodka* are $OBJs_2$ and thus have priority over any other NPs (in this case, *Harry* and *George*) with regard to analyzability as OBJ*(believe)*. But Pr/*like* supersedes either *Fred* or *vodka*, since it is a larger unit containing both — this supersession being determined by the Second Maximization Principle. Hence, Pr/*like* is OBJ*(believe)*; by the Similarity Constraint, *George* is SUBJ*(believe)*, being more similar to *believe* than *Harry*. Consequently, at this point we have:

(21) HARRY KNOW GEORGE BELIEVE FRED LIKE VODKA

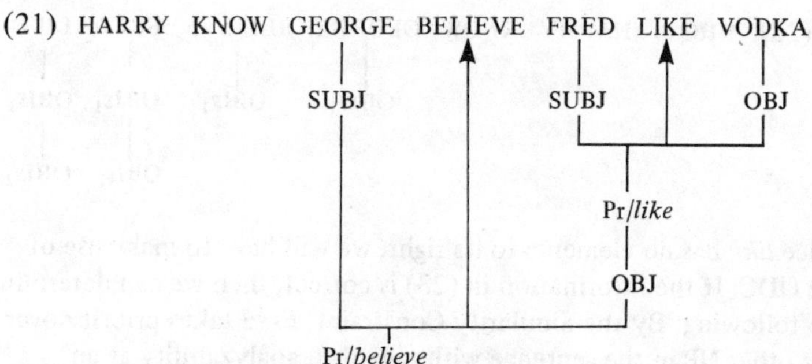

The remainder of the analysis follows in exactly analogous fashion: The NPs *George, Fred,* and *vodka* are all OBJs$_1$ and thus have priority of analyzability as OBJ*(know)* over *Harry*; but Pr/*believe* outranks all of these smaller contained elements and is thus determined to be OBJ*(know)* by the Second Maximization Principle. This leaves *Harry* as the only unanalyzed NP in the sentence, but *know* still requires a Subject; hence, *Harry* is SUBJ*(know)*, and the analysis is completed without violation. (The complete analysis is shown in (2b).)

3.2.2.2. *Non-Normal Form.* In this subsection we will consider discontinuous PRMs, using the following as our paradigm:

(22) a. Who did Harry know that George believed that Fred liked?
      b. Who did Harry know that George believed liked Fred?

The three central principles of|§3.2.1 apply to cases like this just as they do in normal form situations. In other words, there is a uniform system of domain restrictions which handles both kinds of cases. The difference is that in cases involving discontinuity, there is no such simple step-by-step procedure as there was in the normal form case for building up analyses; in showing how the theory applies to sentences like those in (22) we must adopt a more indirect approach. Recall, however, that what is at issue is the completed analysis itself and the means by which it is justified, not the route by which it was obtained; our theory is concerned with possible analyses, not with possible procedures for constructing analyses. (This is merely an alternative way of saying that we do not have an algorithm for analysis, though we do have a way of deciding whether a given analysis is correct.)

Let us now examine (22a). Maximal application of the OR yields

(23) WHO ... HARRY KNOW GEORGE BELIEVE FRED LIKE

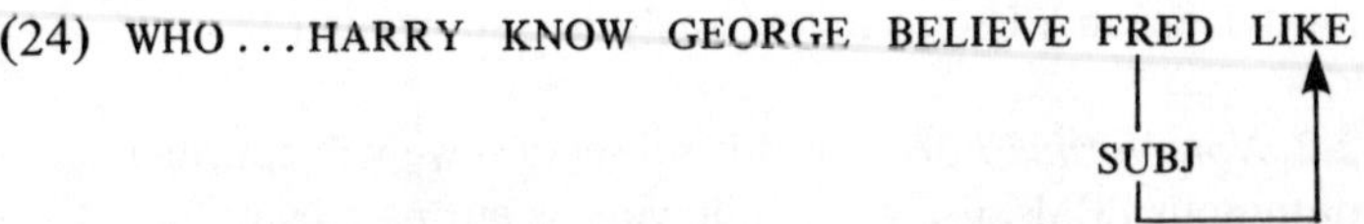

$$OBJs_1 \qquad OBJs_1 \qquad OBJs_1 \quad OBJs_1$$
$$OBJs_2 \quad OBJs_2$$

Since *like* has no elements to its right, we will have to make use of the ODC. If the information in (23) is correct, then we can determine the following: By the Similarity Constraint, *Fred* takes priority over any other NP in the sentence with regard to analyzability as an argument of *like*; moreover, since we know that all arguments of *like* must be to its left, then *Fred* can only be SUBJ*(like)* because, no matter which other NP gets selected as the other argument, only such a result will permit the ODC to be satisfied. That is, regardless of whether we take the pair (*George, Fred*), (*Harry, Fred*), or (*who, Fred*) as arguments of *like*, the ODC will require that these be interpreted as OBJ-SUBJ. Hence, we may posit the following:

(24) WHO ... HARRY KNOW GEORGE BELIEVE FRED LIKE

SUBJ

We are now ready to undertake a search for OBJ*(like)*. Seemingly, it must be *George*, since this is the next most similar NP to *like*. But this choice is empirically incorrect; the actual Object of *like* is *who*. This is in seeming contradiction to the theory, although, in point of fact, the contradiction is only apparent. Let us first show that the theory will block the choice of *George* as OBJ*(like)*. If Pr/*like* is presumed to be manifested by *George* . . . *Fred like,* then this predication must, by the Second Maximization Principle, be OBJ*(believe)*; moreover, either *George* or *Fred* must be SUBJ*(believe)*, since these are both more similar in status to *believe* than either *who* or *Harry*. Hence, the analysis up to this point must be

(25) WHO ... HARRY KNOW GEORGE BELIEVE FRED LIKE

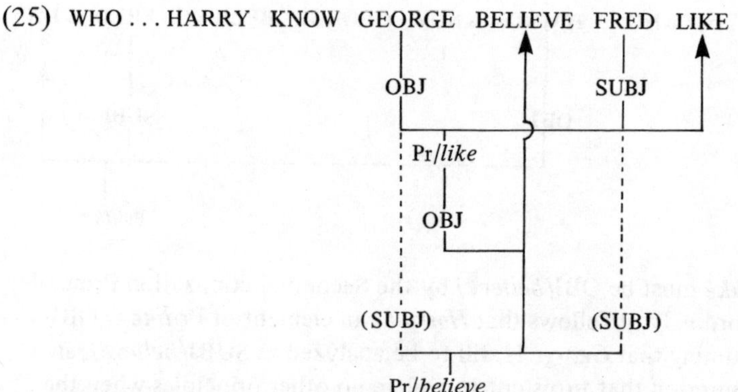

where the broken lines and parenthesized relational labels indicate that either choice could be made for SUBJ*(believe)*. Which choice actually is made is of no consequence, however, since there turns out to be no way to complete the analysis successfully in any case. However constituted, Pr/*believe* will, by the Second Maximization Principle, have to be OBJ*(know)*; this leaves two candidates for SUBJ*(know)*, i.e., *who* and *Harry*. By Uniqueness-b it cannot be both, but by Correspondence neither can be left unanalyzed. Hence, there is no way, given (25) simultaneously to satisfy these two metaconditions in the final analysis. We can trace this result directly to the choice of *George* as OBJ*(like)* and thus rule *George* ineligible to be so analyzed.

The upshot of the foregoing is to establish that the role of OBJ*(like)* must be fulfilled by either *who* or *Harry,* since these are the only remaining NPs. (*George* may still be analyzed as SUBJ*(believe)* without violation in the final analysis. This in turn means that either *who* or *Harry* must also be SUBJ*(know)*.) This might appear to violate the Similarity Constraint, since *George* is more similar to *like* than either *who* or *Harry,* but recall that relative similarity is significant, by the constraint, only for elements which are eligible to be analyzed as $a(P_i)$; since we have just determined that *George* is ineligible to be analyzed as OBJ*(like),* its status is irrelevant. Since no NPs not already accounted for are any more similar to *like* than *who* or *Harry,* either of these NPs can now be considered in principle.

The final choice follows easily from the ODC via the following chain of reasoning. Suppose, again counter to fact, that *Harry* is OBJ*(like)*; we thus obtain

(26) WHO ... HARRY KNOW GEORGE BELIEVE FRED LIKE

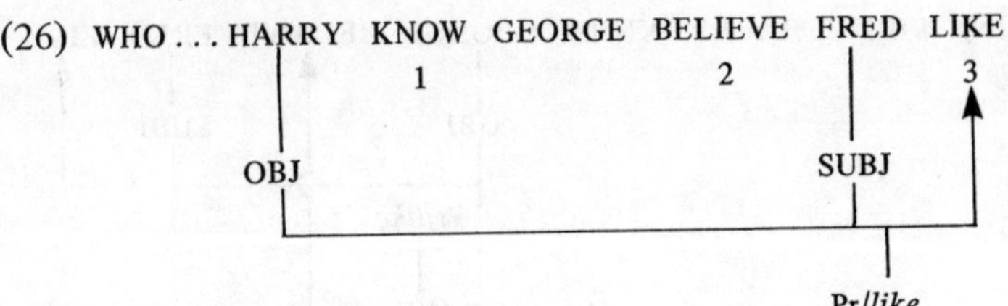

Pr/*like* must be OBJ*(believe)* by the Second Maximization Principle; accordingly, it follows that *Harry* as an element of Pr/*like* is OBJs$_2$. Assuming that *George* is still to be analyzed as SUBJ*(believe)*, an assumption that turns out to violate no other principles when the analysis has been completed, we complete Pr/*believe*; this predication in turn must be OBJ*(know)*, again by the Second Maximization Principle. We thus ultimately obtain:

(27) WHO ... HARRY KNOW GEORGE BELIEVE FRED LIKE

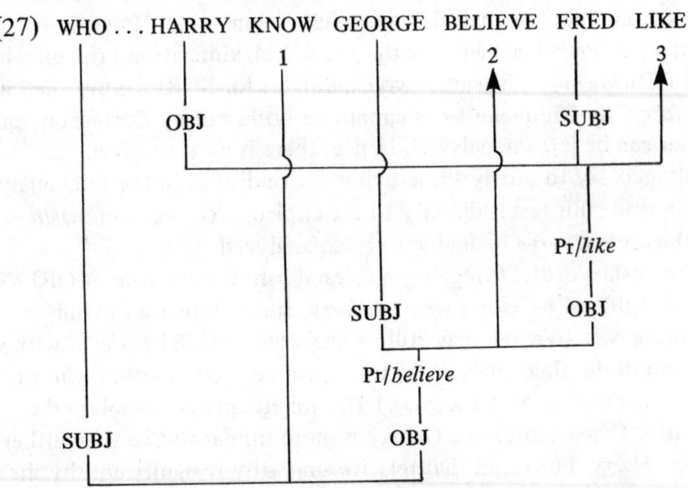

But this result turns out to violate the ODC. If *Harry* is included in Pr/*like,* then it is necessarily also included in Pr/*believe*; but since Pr/*believe* is OBJ*(know)*, then *Harry* is thus OBJs$_1$. *Who,* by virtue of being SUBJ*(know)*, is perforce SUBJs$_1$ and we thus have

(28) WHO ... HARRY KNOW

in which the argument segments with respect to *know* are in the wrong order. If, on the other hand, we choose *who* as OBJ*(like)*, then *Harry* must be SUBJ*(know)*, and the correct result is obtained given the ODC:

(29) WHO ... HARRY   KNOW
      | | 1
      OBJs$_1$ SUBJs$_1$

This analysis satisfies the ODC for all three predicates:

(30) WHO ... HARRY   KNOW   GEORGE   BELIEVE   FRED   LIKE
      | | 1   2   3
      OBJs$_1$----SUBJs$_1$

      OBJs$_2$----------------SUBJs$_2$

      OBJs$_3$-----------------------------------SUBJs$_3$

The overall strategy for dealing with the sentence (and with any analogue thereof) boils down to two steps: (a) demonstrating the ineligibility of a particular NP (in this case, *George*) to enter into the discontinuously manifested predication and (b) selection of the correct element on the basis of the ODC. In so doing, we make use of a quite simple set of principles whose motivation for dealing with simplex sentences and normal form complement constructions is already established. In the example now under discussion, the Similarity Constraint was shown to be irrelevant; it WILL, however, be relevant to more complex cases such as

(31) Samantha wondered *who Harry know George believed Fred liked.*

where the *italicized* segment corresponds to (22a). Within this segment the procedure is exactly the same and yields the same result; since an acceptable result could have been obtained taking *Samantha* as OBJ*(like)*, however, this NP must also be considered eligible, and the Similarity Constraint will come into play to block such a choice.

Lest there be misunderstanding on this point, it should be emphasized that the rather complicated reasoning applied to analyzing a sentence such as this does not imply that the theory itself is complex; indeed, just the contrary is true. Longer and less direct proofs are a natural consequence of simpler axiomatic systems; shortening of proofs requires that additonal axioms (which may actually be theorems of a simpler system) be added. (Compare, for example, the Russell-Whitehead axiomatization of propositional logic, which has only two rules of inference, with more complex systems that add further rules; the former is more elegant, though it generates longer proofs.) At this point our goal is to show that there are certain regularities in surface structure despite the existence of discontinuity of PRMs; these regularities are reflected in the fact that a single set of principles, motivated both for normal and for non-normal form cases, can be given — i.e., that once the correct set of surface structure correlates is identified (the correlates being expressed in terms of argument segment status and relative order of elements), the same principles that apply to normal form cases extend also to non-normal form. A valid performance model, of course, would no doubt employ a rich array of additional principles as heuristic shortcuts; for example, we could considerably shorten the series of steps leading to an analysis of a non-normal form sentence by adding the following:

(32)   In a configuration of the form NP_1-X-NP_2-P_1-. . . - P_i, where no more than one element between P_1 and P_i is eligible to be an argument of P_i, NP_1 must be m-ARG(P_i).

But this principle is itself deducible from independently motivated conditions already established; since this would have to be shown in any case, we would have had to go through precisely the same steps employed in dealing with sentences such as (22a), (31), and so on. It is logically possible that (32) might be a valid perceptual strategy (although see §6.2.1); but such a strategy would work only if a certain type of structural generalization held, and it is precisely the nature of this generalization that we have been attempting to expose by adhering strictly to such independently motivated principles as the Similarity Constraint and the ODC. The relationship of the principles presented here to a psychologically real model of syntactic processing may be conceived of as follows: In order to identify certain regularities in syntactic structure, we have had to assume that certain parameters are relevant to the specification of this structure (segment status being one of the more significant ones); a psychological model must proceed on the basis of some prior commitment to a set of assumptions about what the relevant parameters are. Such a commitment, in turn, can be made in a principled way only on the basis of the predictive and explanatory potency of a linguistic theory which defines the parameters to begin with. For additional discussion of the question of relating purely linguistic and psychological theories of linguistic competence and performance, see §6.2.1 of this study and Kac 1974b.

We now turn to (22b) for which the initial information is

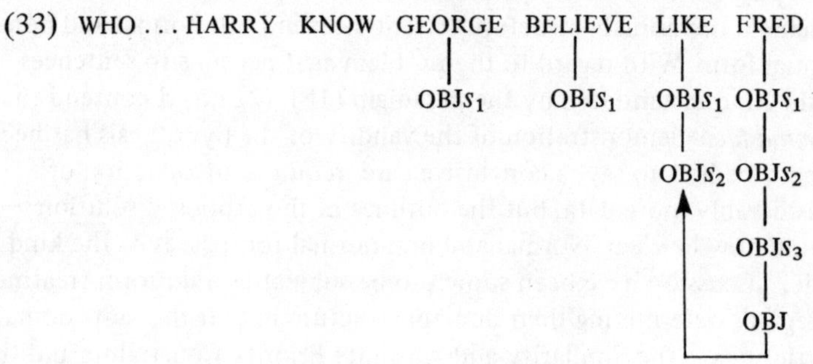

The problem now is to locate a Subject for *like* rather than an Object; aside from this, nothing changes. *George* will have to be rejected as a possibility, as before, since either *who* or *Harry* will have to be left unanalyzed if it is chosen. If, however, *who* is determined to be $OBJs_1$ by the ODC, then the correct result may be obtained. Whereas the ODC does not enter into the determination of the relational interpretation of Pr/*like*, as it did in the previous case, it is none the less relevant to both Pr/*believe* and Pr/*know*, just as before. By virtue of its member-ship in Pr/*like, who* must be $OBJs_2$, since Pr/*like* is OBJ/*believe*). Thus we have the configuration

(34) WHO ... GEORGE BELIEVE ...
$OBJs_2$ $SUBJs_2$ 2

Similarly, with regard to *know* we have the configuration

(35) WHO ... HARRY KNOW ...
$OBJs_1$ $SUBJs_1$ 1

The stipulation that *Harry* is SUBJ/*like)* will be incorrect, since it would lead to the configuration

(36) WHO . . . HARRY KNOW . . .

$\quad\quad$ SUBJs_1 $\quad$ OBJs_1 $\quad\quad\quad$ 1

in violation of the ODC.

Let us take a moment to review what has been accomplished. Our main purpose was to show that a single set of principles would suffice to handle the domain structure of sentences in both normal and non-normal form. With regard to the problem as it pertains to sentences of the kind instantiated by the paradigm (18), (22a,b), I contend that a *prima facie* demonstration of the validity of the hypothesis has been given. Needless to say, a conclusive case requires introduction of considerably more data, but the outlines of the proposed solution should now be clear. Normal and non-normal form cases of the kind under discussion have been shown to be subject to a uniform treatment as regards determining their domain structure in that the same domain restrictions — the Similarity and Absolute Priority Constraints and the Second Maximization Principle — apply to both. The differences have to do with the C-rules involved (the ODC being applicable to the non-normal form cases but not to the normal form ones) and the 'transparency' of the analyses in terms of the steps that must be gone through to obtain them. These differences, however, are irrelevant to the main point at issue, since they do not pertain to domain structure *per se*; they have no effect on determining what kinds of categorial configurations can be predicate domains. Our claim is that in both normal and non-normal form, predicate domains consist of collections of elements having a certain property defined in terms of the notion of status; the linear or hierarchical arrangement of these elements relative to each other is of no consequence with regard to the capacity to possess the relevant property, and hence reference to S-node hierarchies in categorial structure is not necessary in order for predicate domains to be correctly specified.

The method just outlined will, moreover, be applicable regardless of the length of the string which intervenes between elements of a discontinuous PRM. A formal demonstration of this fact will not be given here, though it can be shown informally as follows: Take any structure of the form

$$(37)\quad \text{NP-NP-P-X-} \quad \left\{ \begin{array}{c} \text{NP-P} \\[1em] \text{P-NP} \\ 5 \end{array} \right.$$

$$\quad\quad\quad\quad 1 \quad 2 \ 3 \ 4$$

where X consists solely of NP-P sequences.

Thus (37) schematizes

NP-NP-P-NP-P
NP-NP-P-NP-P-NP-P
NP-NP-P-NP-P-NP-P-NP-P

:

and

NP-NP-P-P-NP
NP-NP-P-NP-P-P-NP
NP-NP-P-NP-P-NP-P-P-NP

:

It will be the case that for any instance of the schema (37), Correspondence and Uniqueness will be able to be simultaneously satisfied only if one of the initial NPs (i.e., 1 or 2) is taken as an argument of the predicate in 5. The choice will be further limited to 1 via the ODC.

3.2.2.3. *Persuade and Related Predicates.* The discussion thus far has not taken into account such verbs as *persuade, advise, inform,* and others which appear to take both elementary and predicational Objects simultaneously. Given a sentence like

(38)   Harry persuaded Fred that he should leave.

we are faced with the following situation: If we consider both *Fred* and Pr/*leave* as manifested by *he should leave* in (38) to be Objects of *persuade,* then we have an apparent violation of the Law of Uniqueness. On the other hand, we might legitimately question the claim that there is a single relation which holds between both arguments of *persuade.* One could, for example, decide that *Fred* is a 'Direct Object' and Pr/*leave* an 'Indirect Object'.

If it were decided that both *Fred* and Pr/*like* should be considered to bear the same relation to *persuade,* the Law of Uniqueness would have to be slightly modified. Specifically, we would amend it to read as follows:

(39)   LAW OF UNIQUENESS – Revised Formulation

a. Unchanged.

b. No two elements in a sentence may be analyzed as bearing the same predicate-argument relation to a single predicate unless they are coordinate, coreferential, OR ARE NOT BOTH a-PREDICATIONAL.

where 'a' is here used in the familiar way as a variable ranging over '+' and '−'. What the added mitigating condition allows is a situation in which two arguments may be in the same relation to a predicate if one is elementary and the other predicational; what is disallowed, except under coordination or coreference, is a situation in which two elementary or two predicational entities are both analyzed as bearing the same relation to a predicate.

Which of the two alternatives under consideration should be taken with regard to predicates like *persuade* must at present be considered an open question. My own intuitive preference is for the latter, making use of the modified formulation of Uniqueness-b, but this is strictly a matter of feel; at the moment, I can see no empirical difference between the two strategies.

3.2.3. *Unmarked Argument Complementation*

3.2.3.1. *Normal Form.* We now turn to the treatment of sentences with Subject or other unmarked argument complements, e.g.,

(40) a. That Harry liked vodka annoyed Maxine.
b. That Harry liked vodka was known by Fred.

In (40a) Pr/*like* acts as SUBJ*(annoy)*; in (40b) Pr/*like* is OBJ*(know)* but still an unmarked argument, since *know* occurs in passive form.

Strictly speaking, our definition of normal form also applies to complement constructions which would, in transformational terms, be said to have undergone 'extraposition':

(41) a. It annoyed Maxine that Harry liked vodka.
b. It was known by Fred that Harry liked vodka.

The reason is that all PRMs are continuous in such constructions.

The principles by which the passives (40b), (41b) would be handled are exactly the same as those by which the actives (40a), (41a) are treated; hence we will confine ourselves here to consideration of the active cases. For purposes of discussion, we will set up the following paradigm:

(42)   a. That Harry liked vodka annoyed Maxime.
       b. That Harry believed the truth annoyed Maxine.
       c. *Harry liked vodka annoyed Maxine.
       d. Harry believed the truth annoyed Maxine.

Two central facts are of interest here: that (42a) is grammatical while (42c) is not and that (42b,d), while both grammatical, have different meanings. It has been frequently noted that complementizers are not dispensable in unmarked argument complements, whereas they may be (given the correct choice of superordinate verb) in marked argument complements. We will offer a proposed explanation of this fact, differing from the standard one (see Bever 1970, Langacker 1974), later in the chapter (§3.2.5). For the moment, our main concern will be with the domain problem as it pertains to (42a, b).

The most interesting way of approaching the problem involves cases like (42b), about which we must ask the following question: What prevents us from applying the principles of the previous section, thus obtaining an analysis according to which (42b) is synonymous with (42d)? The answer, obviously, is that the *that*-complementizer in (42b) works in some way to prevent such a result. Complementizers in general have the function of indicating that the predicates with which they are associated cannot be construed as main predicates. (The conditions under which it is determined that a given complementizer is associated with a given predicate will be made explicit shortly.) Another important observation to be made is that while the method for identifying marked argument complements and of determining the relations of subordination in marked argument complement constructions depends crucially on C-rules — especially the OR — unmarked argument complements cannot be treated in this way, since there are no analogues to the OR for such arguments. In dealing with marked argument complements, we can determine relations of subordination from prior information concerning segment status; in identifying unmarked argument complements, as we will see, it is necessary to do just the reverse — to first determine relations of subordination and then decide how segment status is to be assigned where it is relevant.

The first step in solving the problem is to define the conditions under which a given predicate is associated with (or 'marked by') a particular complementizer. With *to* and *-ing* complementizers, this is easy enough; the former immediately precedes the predicate with which it is associated,

the latter immediately follows. The *that*-complementizer operates somewhat differently, in accordance with the following rule:

(43) *that*-COMPLEMENTIZER MARKING RULE
Analyze the rightmost *that*-complementizer not yet associated
with any predicate as associated with the leftmost unanalyzed
predicate to its right.

where 'unanalyzed predicate' here means 'predicate not yet associated
with a complementizer'. We illustrate with the following example:

(44) It annoyed Harry that it bothered Fred that George came.
                         1   2

Initially, the rightmost complementizer not associated with any
predicate is *that*-2. The leftmost unanalyzed predicate to its right
is *came*. Once *that*-2 is accounted for, *that*-1 is the rightmost complementizer not associated with a predicate, and the leftmost verb
to its right is *bothered*. Thus the associations are as shown in (45):

(45) It annoyed Harry that it bothered Fred that George came.
                         1   2

Now consider the following sentence, predicationally equivalent to
(44):

(46) That that George came bothered Fred annoyed Harry.
          1   2

Such sentences are rather difficult to process but cannot be considered
genuinely ill-formed. Here we begin once again by linking *that*-2, the
rightmost complementizer, to a predicate; the leftmost predicate to the
right is *came*. Then we link up *that*-1 with the next leftmost unanalyzed
predicate to the right, namely, *bothered*:

(47) That that George came bothered Fred annoyed Harry.
          1   2

Self-embedding cases like (46) show the need for specifying 'leftmost
unanalyzed predicate to the right' rather than simply 'leftmost
unanalyzed predicate'; the latter would be sufficient for (44) but not
for (46).

A similar type of rule holds for the *for-to*-complementizer, as follows:

(48) *for-to*-COMPLEMENTIZER RULE
   a. Analyze the rightmost *for* not yet associated with any
      predicate as associated with the leftmost unanalyzed
      predicate to its right.
   b. For every predicate associated with a *for,* a *to* must
      immediately precede the predicate.

We now state the principle for associating complementizer marking
with subordinate status:

(49) COMPLEMENTIZER MARKING INTERPRETATION
      PRINCIPLE
      If P is marked by a complementizer, Pr/P may not be
      construed as the main predication of the sentence in which
      it appears.

Finally, we specify precisely how relative subordination is to be determined in situations where complementizer marking is involved:

(50) RELATIVE SUBORDINATION RULE
      For any two predicates P_i, P_j marked by complementizers,
      P_i is subordinate to P_j if the complementizer by which P_i
      is marked is to the right of the complementizer by which
      P_j is marked.

Hence, in (45) and in (47), *come* is subordinate to *bother.* Notice that
it is not the order of the predicates themselves that determines relative
subordination but the order of the complementizers associated with
them. The rule in question is not necessarily universal; it seems,
however, to have general applicability in English regardless of
complementizer type.

Let us now analyze (42b), here repeated as

(51) That Harry believed the truth annoyed Maxine.

taking up first the problem of fixing the domain of *believe*. In particular, we must show how (51) is to be distinguished from

(52) Harry believed the truth annoyed Maxine. (=(42d))

Maximal application of the OR to (51) would yield, ultimately, the following result:

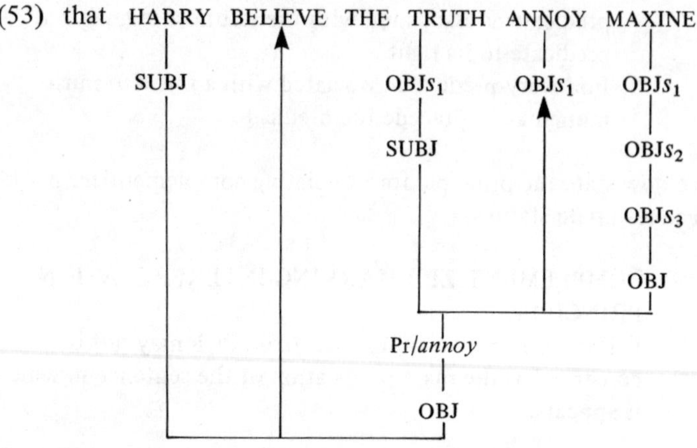

Needless to say, this must be prevented somehow. We can in fact show that maximal application in this case will lead to an invalid result in terms of the theory, as follows: If Pr/*annoy* is OBJ*(believe)*, then Pr/*annoy* is subordinate to Pr/*believe*. Thus *believe* is then the main verb under such an analysis: in (53) it is the predicate which is not subordinate to any other. But *believe* is marked by a *that*-complementizer, whose function it is to indicate that *believe* is NOT the main verb. The conflict may be viewed in another way as follows: If *annoy* is OBJs$_1$, it (and its associated predication) must be subordinate to *believe*; but if, in the sentence in question, *believe* is not the main verb, then it must be subordinate to *annoy*. In other words, the situation is one in which symmetric subordination obtains; but we have defined subordination as an asymmetric relation, and hence such an outcome is impossible.

We are thus forced to the conclusion that *believe* must be subordinate to *annoy*, which means that *annoy* is not eligible to be marked as OBJs$_1$ — since so to mark it is tantamount to stating that Pr/*annoy* is OBJ*(believe)*, which we have already determined to be false. The correct initial information then is

(54) that HARRY BELIEVE THE TRUTH ANNOY MAXINE

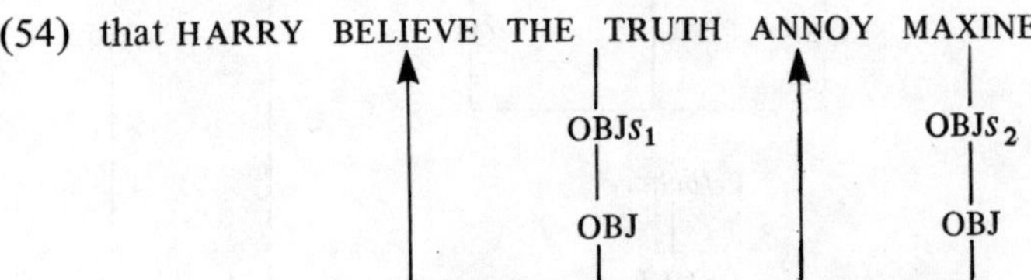

That *the truth* is the only possible candidate for OBJ*(believe)* is determined by a further domain restriction:

(55) LEFT PRIORITY CONSTRAINT
If X and Y are to the right of P and are eligible to be analyzed as *m*-ARG(P), X has priority of analyzability as such over Y if X is to the left of Y.

According to this constraint, *the truth* must be OBJ*(believe)*, since it is to the left of *Maxine* and both are eligible to be so marked. Similarly, in

(56) Harry was believed by Fred to be liked by Maxine.

Fred must be SUBJ*(believe)*, since it is to the left of *Maxine*.

The remainder of the analysis of (51) follows in straightforward fashion. That *Harry* must be SUBJ*(believe)* may be determined as follows: We already know that Pr/*believe* must be subordinate to *annoy*, which in turn means that it must be SUBJ*(annoy)*, since (a) an Object has already been identified and (b) *annoy* takes predicational Subjects but not predicational Objects. Moreover, *the truth* could not be SUBJ*(believe)*, since Uniqueness-a would be violated by such an assumption. This means that the only NP other than *Harry* that could be SUBJ*(believe)* is *Maxine*; but under such an assumption, *Harry* would have to be left unanalyzed, since, as previously established, Pr/*believe*, however constituted, would have to be SUBJ*(annoy)*. Pr/*believe* and Pr/*annoy* would, in other words, have both been completed without *Harry* having been taken into account, leaving it without a role to pay — in violation of Correspondence. Hence, *Harry* must be SUBJ*(believe)*, and the final analysis is

(57) that HARRY BELIEVE THE TRUTH ANNOY MAXINE

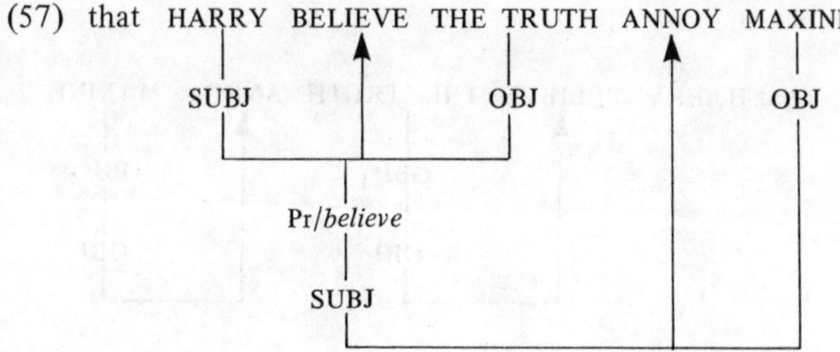

Suppose now that (51) is embedded as a Subject complement in a larger context, as in

(58) *That Harry believed the truth annoyed Maxine* bothered Fred.

where the italics indicate the portion of (58) coinciding with (51). Note that the italic portion nonetheless does not have the same meaning as (51) in isolation, but rather has the meaning of

(59) Harry believed the truth annoyed Maxine. (=(42d))

This switch in meaning is accounted for as follows: Note first that (58) has three predicates but only one complimentizer, marking *believe*. This means that *believe* is not the main verb; but now there are two other possibilities for main verb status rather than just one. In (58), in contrast to (51), *believe* does not have to be subordinate to *annoy,* since it might be construed as subordinate to *bother* even if superordinate to *annoy.* That is, *believe* in (58) need be construed only as subordinate to SOME predicate, not necessarily to *annoy,* since *annoy* is not the only other predicate in the sentence. It can in fact be shown via the First Maximization Principle and Left Priority Constraint that *annoy* must indeed be subordinate to *believe* in (58). The reasoning runs as follows: If we attempt to apply the OR maximally, then both *annoy* and *bother* will end up subordinate to *believe*; but this is impossible, since, by virtue of being marked by a complementizer, *believe* must be subordinate to one or the other of the remaining two verbs. This leaves us with two alternatives, as diagrammed on p. 81.

(60) a. that

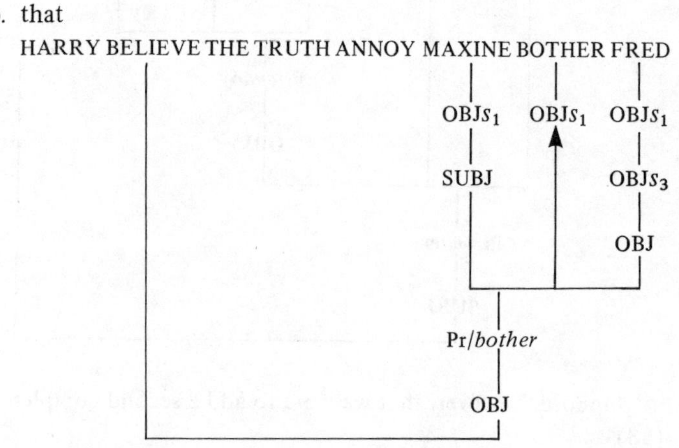

b. that

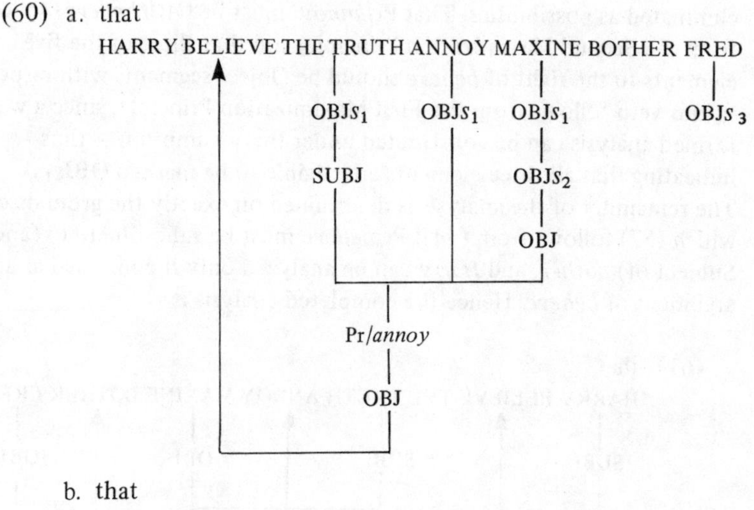

The analysis shown in (60a) results from the decision not to count *bother* or *Fred* as OBJs₁, while that in (60b) results from the decision not to count *the truth* or *annoy*. That (60a) must be selected over (60b) follows from the Left Priority Constraint: Pr/*annoy* as constituted in the former is to the left of Pr/*bother* as constituted in the latter, and hence Pr/*annoy* has priority of analyzability as OBJ*(believe)* over Pr/*bother*. (The Left Priority Constraint is, in other words, here being used as the basis for a decision as to how predications should be constituted; given either possibility, we select the one which places the predicational Object of *believe* further to the left.) We now know that *bother* must be the main verb, since both *believe* and *annoy* are

eliminated as possibilities. That Pr/*annoy* must be OBJ*(believe)* follows from the Second Maximization Principle; and that three of the five elements to the right of *believe* should be Object segments with respect to this verb follows from the First Maximization Principle, since a well-formed analysis can be constructed under this assumption — thus indicating that all three elements are eligible to be marked OBJs$_1$.
The remainder of the analysis is determined on exactly the grounds on which (57) follows from (54): Pr/*believe* must be subordinate to (and Subject of) *bother*, and *Harry* can be analyzed only if construed as an argument of *believe.* Hence the completed analysis is

(61)   that

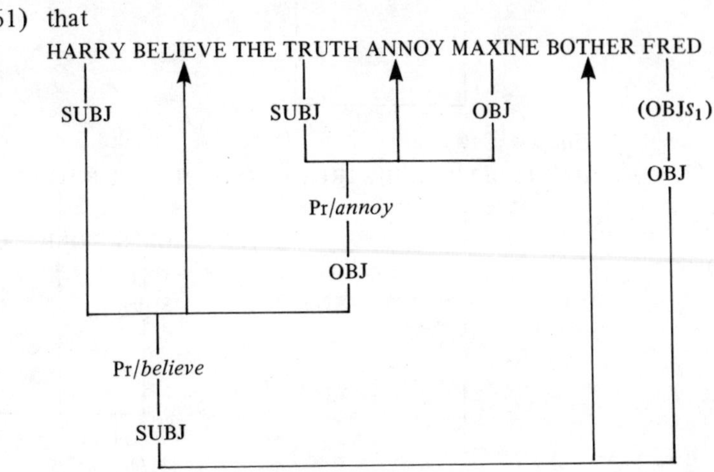

Suppose, however, that we were to add a second complementizer to (58)

(62)   *That that Harry believed the truth annoyed Maxine* bothered Fred.

where the italic portion now consists of a string corresponding to the italic portion of (58) but with an additional *that*-complementizer at the beginning. With this addition, the meaning of the italic segment switches back to the meaning of

(63)   That Harry believed the truth annoyed Maxine. (=(51))

That is, (62) has, rather than (61), the following analysis:

(64) that that
      1   2

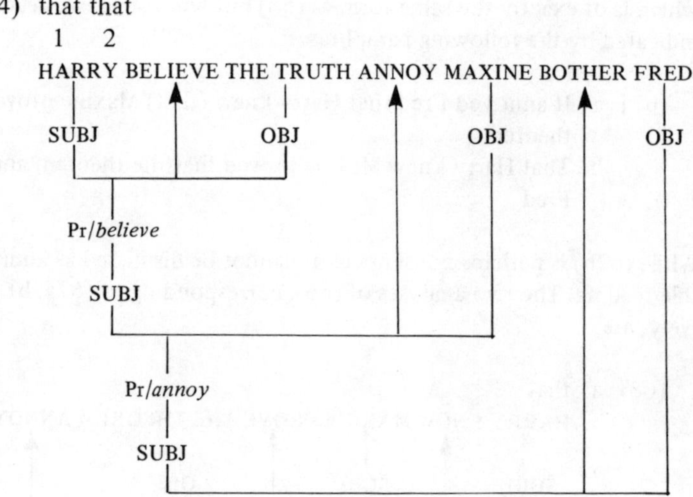

The reason is quite apparent: Once the second *that* is added, the complementizer marking structure is as follows:

(65) that that Harry believed the truth annoyed Maxine . . .
      1   2

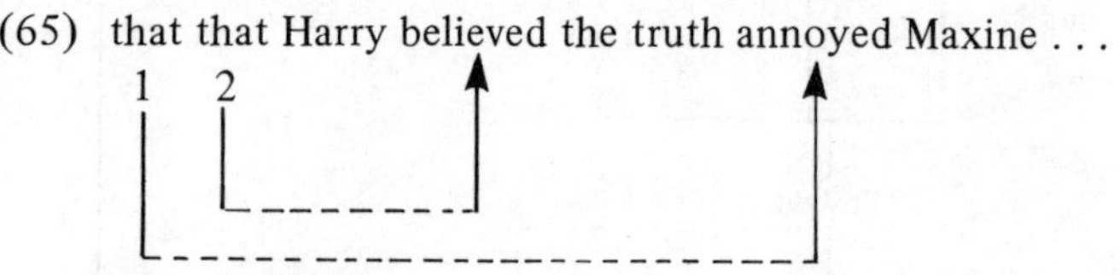

By the Relative Subordination Rule (see (50) above), *believe* must here be subordinate to *annoy*; consequently, neither *annoy* nor *bother* can be OBJs$_1$ in (62), which can only mean that Pr/*believe* is SUBJ(*annoy*) just as it is in (63).

We now raise the following question: It is the fact that *annoy* may take both predicational and elementary Subjects while *believe* can take both predicational and elementary Objects that is responsible for the behavior of these predicates in the constructions just discussed. Suppose we now consider a predicate like *prove*, which may take both predicational or elementary arguments in BOTH the Subject and Object relations. With such a predicate we might expect to get ambiguities in certain constructions; is this expectation realized? The answer is affirmative. Consider

(66) That Harry knew Maxine proved the theorem annoyed Fred.

which is of exactly the same form as (58) but which has two readings as indicated by the following paraphrases:

(67) a. It annoyed Fred that Harry knew (that) Maxine proved the theorem.
   b. That Harry knew Maxine proved that the theorem annoyed Fred.

While (67b) is perhaps nonsensical, it cannot be dismissed as an impossible reading. The two analyses of (66), corresponding to (67a, b) respectively, are

(68) a. that

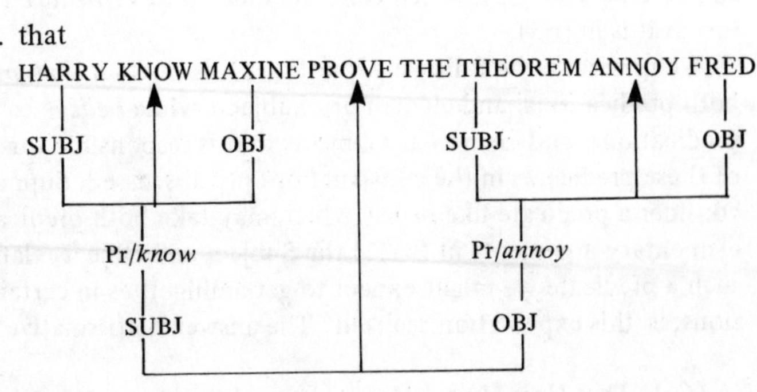

(Compare (61).)

   b. that
HARRY KNOW MAXINE PROVE THE THEOREM ANNOY FRED
SUBJ   OBJ   SUBJ   OBJ
Pr/know   Pr/annoy
SUBJ   OBJ

The ambiguity is a result of an interaction between *prove* and *know* as regards the results required by the First Maximization Principle. If the principle is applied first with respect to *know,* the result is as shown in (68a) analogous to the analysis of (58) shown in (61). If, on the other hand, the principle is applied first with respect to *prove*, then all elements to its right must be Object segments with respect to it. This leads ultimately to analyzing Pr/*annoy* as constituted in (68b) as OBJ*(prove)*. Since *know* must be subordinate to some predicate and since *annoy* has already been determined not to have any predicational arguments, Pr/*know* can only be subordinate to *prove.* To account for *Harry* and *Maxine* so as to satisfy Correspondence, both NPs must be presumed part of Pr/*know*; the remainder of the analysis follows simply once these points are established.

In sum, the eligibility of NPs for marking as Object segments relative to *know* and *prove* is affected by which verb is considered first. If *know* is taken first, then satisfaction of the First Maximization Principle relative to this predicate requires the result shown in (68a) with a concomitant reduction in the number of elements eligible to be Object segments relative to *prove*; but if *prove* is considered first, then satisfaction of the First Maximization Principle has the result shown in (68b) and the number of possible Object segments relative to *know* is reduced. It is the trade-off relation between the two predicates in this context which is responsible for the ambiguity.

Let us now consider the unambiguous sentence (67a) to illustrate the treatment of extraposed constructions. Recall from Chapter 2 that the 'expletive *it*' which occurs in such constructions is one of the class of NPs which do not have to be analyzed as arguments of predicates. The analysis of (67a) proceeds as follows: the initial result is

(69) it ANNOY FRED that HARRY KNOW MAXINE PROVE THE THEOREM

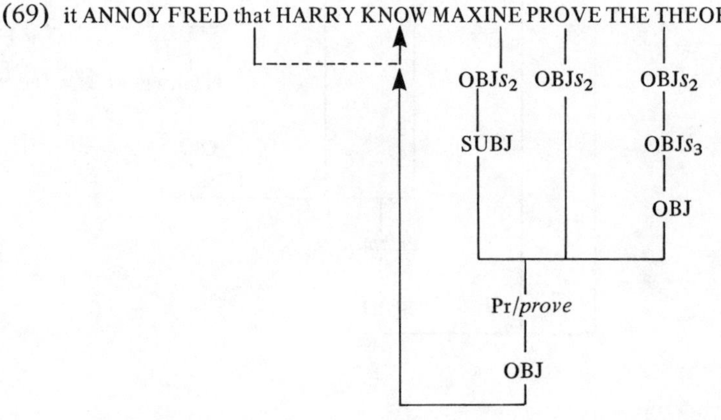

The remainder of the analysis is determined simply from the following considerations: First, it follows from the information in (69) that Pr/*know*, however constituted, must be subordinate to *annoy*, since (a) it must be subordinate to some predicate in the sentence given that it is marked by *that* and (b) it cannot be subordinate to Pr/*prove* given the stricture against symmetric subordination. The determination of SUBJ*(know)* is accomplished via the Left Priority Constraint: If *Harry* is SUBJ*(know)*, then *Fred* must be OBJ*(annoy)*; and if *Fred* is SUBJ*(know)*, then *Harry* must be OBJ*(annoy)*:

(70)   . . . ANNOY FRED . . . HARRY KNOW . . .

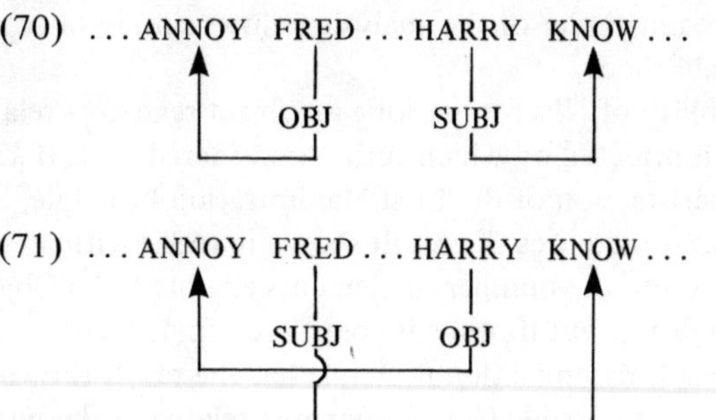

(71)   . . . ANNOY FRED . . . HARRY KNOW . . .

Since *Fred* is to the left of *Harry*, the former has priority of analyzability as OBJ*(annoy)* over the latter, and (70) is the correct alternative. Thus the complete analysis is

(72) it ANNOY FRED that HARRY KNOW MAXINE PROVE THE THEOREM

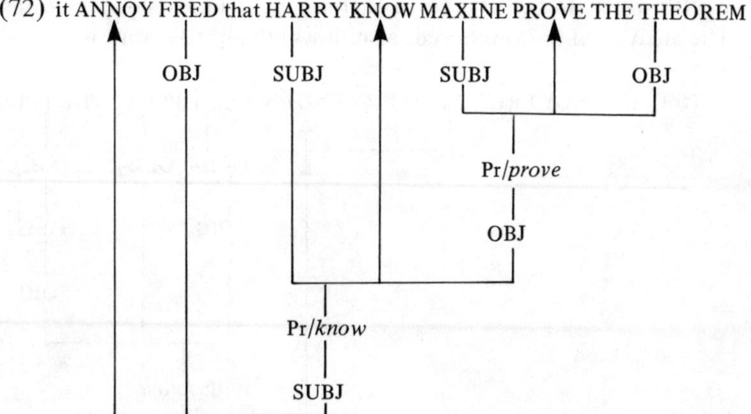

3.2.3.2. *Non-Normal Form.* We conclude this portion of the presentation with a discussion of the following example in non-normal form:

(73) Maxine was believed by Harry to be thought by George to like Fred.

The initial result will be

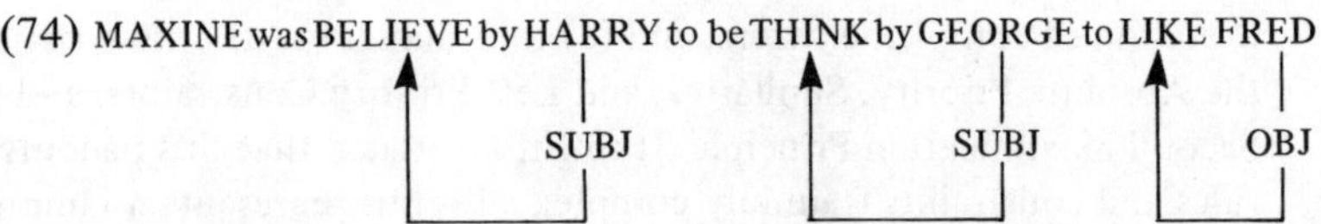

The rule for associating *to*-complementizers with predicates is a simple one, requiring that *to* be associated with the verb to its immediate right. By the Relative Subordination Rule, *like* is subordinate to *think*; since *think* must itself be subordinate to some predicate, *believe* must be the main verb.

Pr/*like*, however constituted, must be OBJ*(think)*; since *Maxine* is as yet unaccounted for, it is a natural candidate for SUBJ*(like)*. All C-rules and metaconditions are ultimately satisfied by the analysis

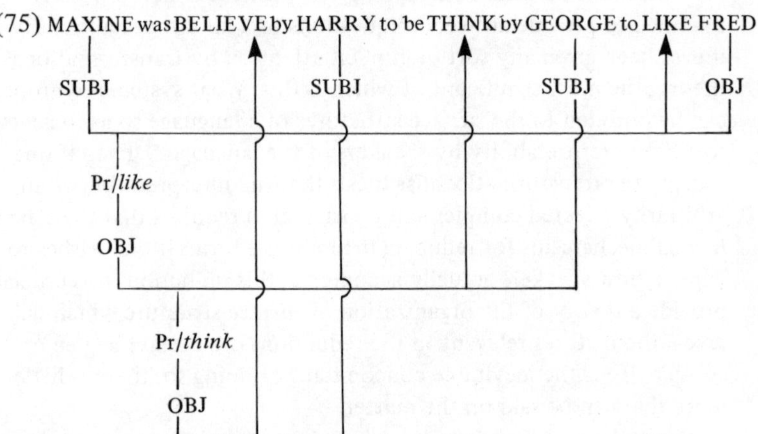

That Pr/*like* is OBJ*(think)* follows because (a) Pr/*like* is, by the Relative Subordination Rule, subordinate to Pr/*think* and (b) *think* takes predicational Objects; that Pr/*think* is subordinate to Pr/*believe* follows for analogous reasons. Thus, non-normal form cases of this types pose no particular difficulties.

3.2.4. *A Necessity Argument*

In §§3.2.1-3.2.3 we outlined the essentials of a solution to the domain problem which involves principles applied directly to surface structure and which makes use of structural information other than that provided by S-node hierarchies of the kind relied on by standard transformational approaches to the problem. Central to the account developed above are (a) the notion 'argument segment' and the use of this notion in stating certain principles of the theory, (b) a set of principles for the interpretation of complementizers, and (c) four domain restrictions, namely, the Absolute Priority, Similarity, and Left Priority Constraints, and the Second Maximization Principle. It might be argued that this panoply of rules and constraints is unduly complex and thus represents no improvement over what it is supposed to replace; but such a view would be mistaken for two reasons. First, the matter of relative complexity of alternative accounts has adjudicative relevance only if the accounts are equivalent in all other respects; I will present evidence below that this *ceteris paribus* prerequisite does not hold when the corepresentational treatment is compared with the standard transformational one. Moreover, in justifying an account the emphasis rightly belongs not on its superficial formal properties but rather on what it reveals about the range of phenomena to which it is addressed. The proposed corepresentational method of analyzing complement constructions is intended to provide answers to questions of a kind that have rarely if ever been given any sort of explicit attention by transformational theory, the most significant of which is this: What systematic properties can be imputed to the surface structures of a language so as to account for their interpretability by speakers of the language?[4] Even if one accepts the transformationalist thesis that the interpretation of an arbitrarily selected complement construction requires that there be some formal mechanisms for reducing it to normal form, if one wishes to explain how speakers actually accomplish this reduction, it is crucial to provide a theory of the organization of surface structure which will reveal the features relevant to the reduction. If a certain degree of complexity is the inevitable concomitant of doing so, there is little more that can be said on the matter.

It may be worthwhile in this connection to reiterate one of the points raised in §3.1.2. It was suggested there that it would be of interest to show that a particular set of principles could handle both normal and non-normal form; in §§3.2.2 and 3.2.3 evidence was presented in favor of this claim, and at least the beginning of a case was made. On the basis of the presentation so far, it can at least be shown that sentences of a kind commonly cited to show the 'necessity' of a prior reduction to normal form if the predicational structure of non-normal form complement constructions is to be captured do not in fact show what they are claimed to. While the principles required for constructions with unmarked argument complements (§3.2.3) are somewhat different from those given for constructions with marked argument complements (§3.2.2), in either type of construction the principles that account for normal form account for non-normal form as well. This at least permits us to advance the interesting claim that non-normal form is not, as commonly supposed, 'degenerate' in not adhering to a particular, supposedly 'ideal' type of structural arrangement but represents, rather, an alternative arrangement wholly consistent with the constraints obeyed by normal form constructions.

At this point, I wish to consider a problem in the analysis of complement constructions which has a natural solution given the principles developed in this chapter but does not given the usual assumptions about complementation in standard transformational grammar. Whereas we have previously been concerned with showing that it is POSSIBLE to construct a certain kind of alternative account, we will now be attempting to show that it is NECESSARY to do so. More specifically, we will argue for the necessity of the assumption that categorial representations do not contain S-nodes and that something other than the hierarchical relationships among Ss in categorial structure must be taken as determining how a description of predicational structure will be assigned. Since the corepresentational account developed above turns out to be sufficient to explain the relevant facts, whereas the standard transformational account is not, we will have grounds for preferring the former.

We begin by reconsidering (42b, d), here repeated as

(76)   a. That Harry believed the truth annoyed Maxine.
       b. Harry believed the truth annoyed Maxine.

to which the conventional theory of complementation would assign the following structures:

(77)   a.

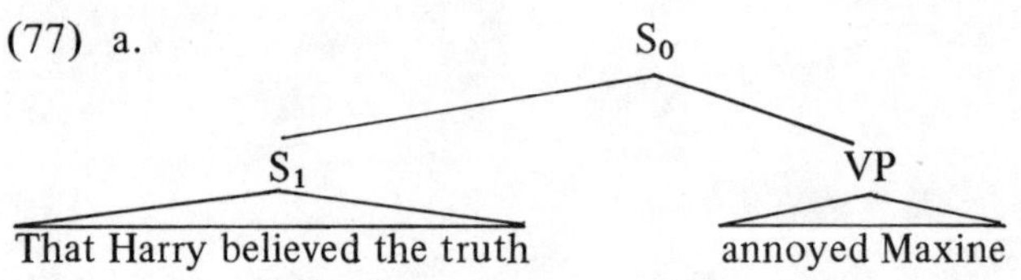

b.

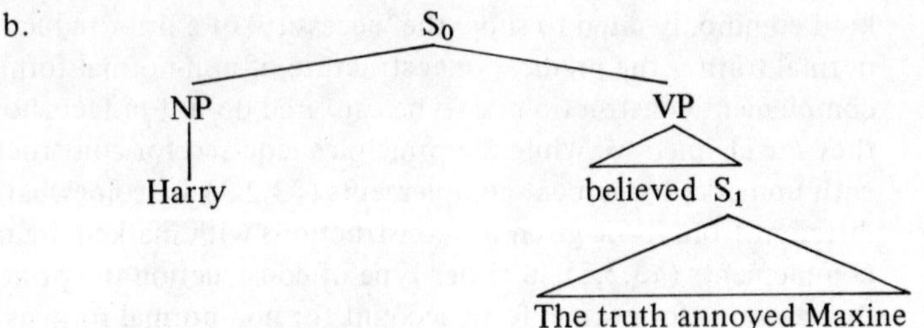

Since *that*-complementizers are obligatory with Subject complements, the *that* in (76a) may be taken as a cue to the effect that an embedded clause follows; in the absence of any complementizer, the embedded S cannot be presumed to be in Subject position, and (77b) is the only possibility.

Let us now embed (76a) as an Object complement as in

(78) George knows *that Harry believed the truth annoyed Maxine.*

where the italic string corresponds exactly to (76a). A switch in meaning now takes place: The italic segment in (78) no longer has the same meaning as (76a) in isolation, but rather, has the meaning of (76b). Under the usual transformational treatment of complementation, this result is unexpected. What would be predicted, rather, is that (78) should be ambiguous as between readings corresponding to the following P-markers taken as underlying representations:

(79) a.

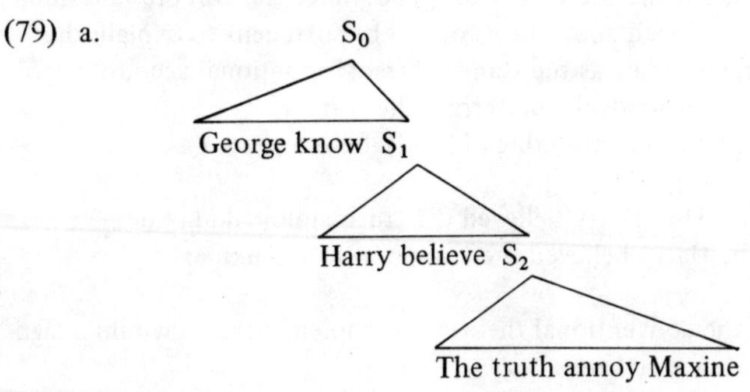

b.

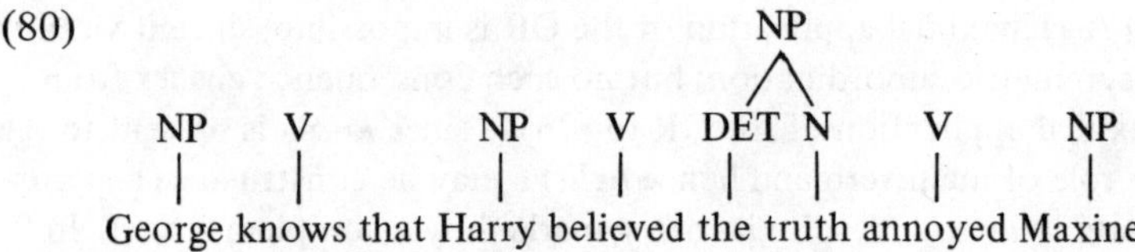

Structure (79a) corresponds to the actual reading of (78) and poses no problem: Since the *that*-complementizer is optional in Object complements, it need not be inserted in S_2 in (79a); if the option is taken to insert it in S_1 then (78) results (after Subject-Verb Argeement) with the correct interpretation. But now consider (79b): Since S_2 is a Subject complement, it must receive a complementizer, in this case a *that*. But S_1 is an Object complement not requiring a complementizer, and thus no *that* need be inserted at this hierarchical level. It is thus also possible to derive (78) with the S-hierarchy (and thus the corresponding reading) of (79b). But (78) does not actually have this meaning as one of its possible senses, and thus the standard account is incorrect in what it predicts.

We are here faced with two interrelated problems. The first is to explain why (78) is unambiguous, counter to our expectations; the second is to explain why it has just the meaning that it has — i.e., why its one actual meaning corresponds to (79a) rather than (79b). In a corepresentational account such as that given in this chapter, the solution is quite straightforward. The categorial representation of the sentence may be given as

(80)

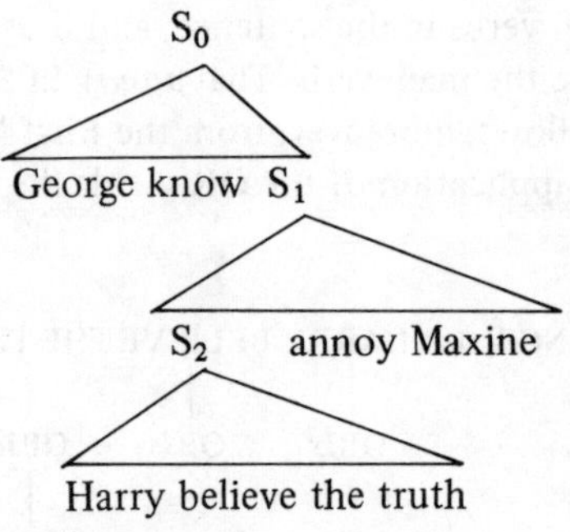

By the *that*-Complementizer Marking Rule, the complementizer is associated with *believe* and thus indicates that it cannot be the main verb. In (76a) this would mean that *annoy* would have to be the main verb, since it is the only other predicate in the sentence. But in (78)

there are TWO other verbs in the sentence, and thus it does not follow
that *annoy* has to be the main verb. That *annoy* in fact CANNOT
be the main verb follows, moreover, from the First Maximization
Principle. Maximal application of the OR yields the result shown in
(81):

(81)   GEORGE KNOW that HARRY BELIEVE THE TRUTH ANNOY MAXINE

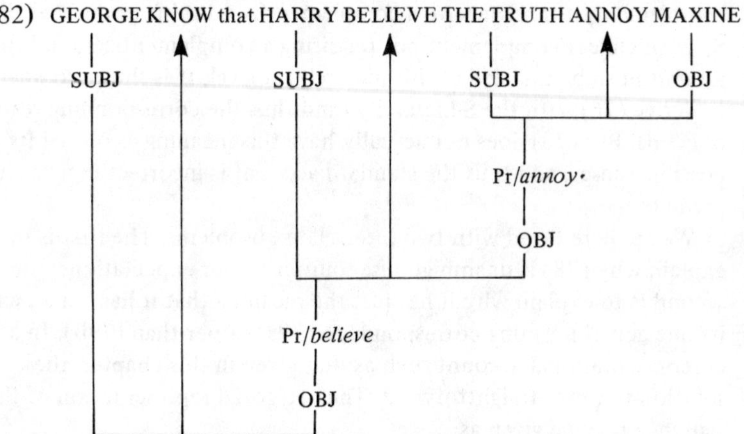

from which follows the well-formed analysis

(82)   GEORGE KNOW that HARRY BELIEVE THE TRUTH ANNOY MAXINE

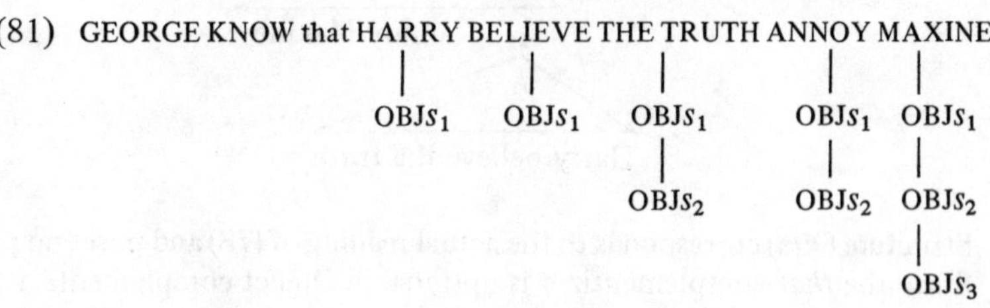

In (76a) maximal application of the OR is impossible, since it would lead
to symmetric subordination; but no such consequence ensues from
maximal application of the OR to (78) — since *know* is present to take
the role of main verb and hence *believe* may be construed as superordinate to *annoy*, despite its being marked by a complementizer. In (78),
because there are three verbs in the sentence, the complementizer
marking on *believe* tells us that this verb is not the main predicate, but
nothing more; there is no necessity that it be regarded as subordinate
to *annoy* if it is subordinate to *know*. Since the analysis (81), consistent
with maximal application of the OR, violates no principle of the theory,

the First Maximization Principle requires that it be selected. That is, since (81) is well-formed, all elements to the right of *know* and *believe* are eligible to be analyzed by the OR as Object segments with respect to these two predicates; under such conditions, according to the First Maximization Principle, they must be so analyzed, and *believe* must therefore be superordinate to *annoy*.

Now compare (78) to

(83) George knows *that that Harry believed the truth annoyed Maxine.*

Here, the italic segment is exactly like that in (78) except that two *that*-complementizers occur at the beginning of the string rather than just one. With the addition of this second *that,* the meaning of the italic segment switches back again to that associated with (76a). This fact is also naturally explained by our account: By the Relative Sub-ordination Rule, applied to the configuration

(84) ... that that Harry believed the truth annoyed Maxine

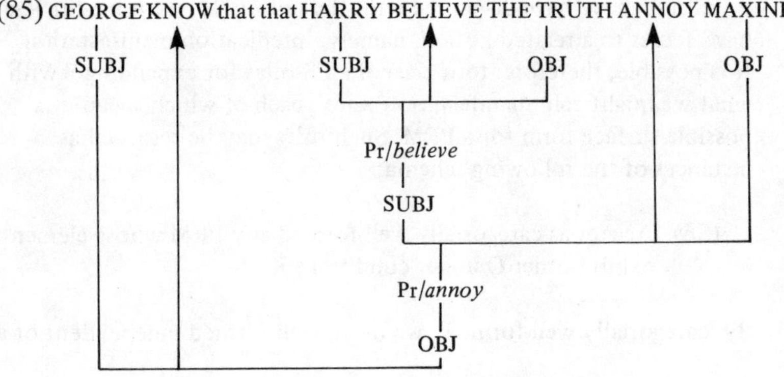

believe must be subordinate to *annoy*, since *that*-2 is to the right of *that*-1. This precludes maximal application of the OR; more specifically, it precludes the elements to the right of *believe* from being taken as Object segments with respect thereto, since symmetric subordination WOULD then ensue within the underscored segment. Hence (83) must have the analysis

(85) GEORGE KNOW that that HARRY BELIEVE THE TRUTH ANNOY MAXINE

The contrast between (78) and (83), in a nutshell, is that the Relative Subordination Rule is applicable only to the latter and not to the former. In (78) the single complementizer indicates only that *believe* is subordinate to SOME predicate, but leaves the decision open as to just how it fits into the overall subordination scheme; that decision then follows from the First Maximization Principle. In (83), by contrast, two complementizers are present, and the Relative Subordination Rule must come into play. The result is that the complementizers give substantially more information about the overall subordination pattern, specifically, that *believe* is subordinate to *annoy*.

Notice that the foregoing does not imply that there are no ambiguities in English as to subordination relations. We have already treated a case of this kind of ambiguity, namely, (66). There, it will be recalled, the First Maximization Principle could be satisfied in either of two ways with concomitant effects elsewhere in the analysis.

Overall, then, I submit that the corepresentational theory of complementation in English exhibits a significant degree of descriptive sensitivity and explanatory power. That it is somewhat complex cannot be denied, but I would contend that the results are worth the cost. This is not to deny, however, that improvements and refinements may well be required; that the search for such improvements and refinements — i.e., active research on corepresentational grammar — is justified by precisely these initial results seems to be a position that could be reasonably advocated.

To conclude this section, I would like to take up a matter left in abeyance in Chapter 1. It was noted there (§1.7) that if S-nodes are no longer recognized in categorial representations, certain well-formedness conditions that would normally be expressed via rules of the form $S \dashrightarrow \ldots$ must be dealt with in some other way. We will now deal with the question of finding an alternative.

Although we have dispensed with the notion 'S', we none the less have access to a related notion, namely, 'predication manifestation'. It is possible, therefore, to replace the PS-rules for expanding S with what we might call 'manifestation rules', each of which specifies a possible surface form for a PRM. Such rules may be regarded as instances of the following schema:

(86)   Accept as categorially well-formed any PRM whose elements exhibit order O under conditions K.

By 'categorially well-formed', we mean well-formed independent of any considerations pertaining to relational structure. So, for example, both (87a) and (87b) are categorially well-formed according to the rule (88), but (87b) is none the less ill-formed on grounds pertaining to relational structure, since the strict subcategorization of the predicate is violated:

(87) a. Vodka, Harry likes.
      b. *Vodka, Harry sleeps.

(88) Accept as categorially well-formed any PRM whose elements exhibit the order NP-NP-V, under conditions . . .

We may take (88) as a statement to the effect that the arguments of a two-place predicate may both precede the predicate. It applies equally to PRMs such as (87a) and the italic sequence in the following:

(89) *Who* does George think *Maxine likes?*

   NP   NP   V

Similarly, the rule (90) is satisfied by the italic sequence in (91):

(90) Accept as categorially well-formed any PRM whose elements exhibit the order NP-V-NP.

(91) *Who* does George think *likes Maxine?*

   NP   V   NP

Included in the conditions for (88) will be some statement to the effect that it does not apply to continuous PRMs in the form NP-NP-V if they occur as complements:

(92) a. *George thinks (that) Fred, Maxine likes.
      b. *That Fred, Maxine likes annoys George.

The problem of stating (and explaining) such restrictions as that which prohibits sentences like those in (92) must, of course, be confronted by any grammatical theory.

The manifestation rules of a corepresentational grammar may be regarded as jointly specifying the 'canonical forms' of PRMs in the language for which the grammar is written. PS-rules may be regarded as having this function for lower-order constituents, with the additional one of imposing certain types of hierarchical structure and accounting for recursion where necessary; so, for example, the PS-rule $N \longrightarrow$ A-N states (a) that adjectival modifiers precede head nouns, (b) that A-N sequences are themselves Ns, and (c) that there are infinitely many Ns of the form A_1- . . . -A_n -N conforming to the structural schema

(93)

$$N \quad [A_1 \ \ldots \ A_n \ N]$$

Manifestation rules do not impose any hierarchization (though elements to which they refer may be hierarchized by PS-rules), nor do they account for recursion. This is the essential difference between such rules and PS-rules.

3.2.5. *Marked and Unmarked Argument Complementation: A Comparison*

In this section we draw together the findings of the preceding ones to construct a unified theory of subordination cues in English. For convenience, let us bring together into a single paradigm some of the basic examples:

(94)   a. Harry believes the truth annoys Maxine.
       b. Harry believes that the truth annoys Maxine.
       c. That Harry believes the truth annoys Maxine.
       d. That Harry likes vodka annoys Maxine.
       e. *Harry likes vodka annoys Maxine.

The sentences in (94) illustrate the well-known asymmetry, previously alluded to, between unmarked and marked argument complements with regard to complementizers. (94a-b) show the optionality of the *that*-complementizer for marked argument complements while (94c-e) show that some sort of complementizer marking is obligatory for unmarked argument complements: (94c) is a paraphrase neither of (94a) nor of (94b), and (94e) is ill-formed.

    A common explanation of the phenomenon in question, reiterated in various places, goes as follows:

> . . . surface structures such as [(94e)] would present the listener with certain processing difficulties; in this instance, the listener would NATURALLY [emphasis

added] hypothesize (mistakenly) that [*Harry likes* . . .] initiates the main clause since nothing would signal subordinate status until later in the sentence. The retention of *that* in a sentence-initial complement clause enables the listener to avoid this processing error; but in sentences like [(94a-b)] where the previous context . . . makes it clear that a following clause will be subordinate, *that* is in a sense superfluous and thus may be omitted. (Langacker 1974, p. 631)

I would agree with the author cited that the asymmetry in the paradigm (94) is to be accounted for in terms of superfluity or redundancy of the complementizer in (94a-b) as opposed to its non-redundancy in (94c-d) — but not for the reasons he gives, which, on close examination, turn out to be not only non-explanatory but empirically erroneous as well. Langacker is here evidently relying on a proposed perceptual strategy (Bever 1970) as follows:

(95) The first N . . . V . . . (N) clause is the main clause unless the verb is marked as subordinate.

This principle is apparently empirically defensible in early child language, but its significance is limited to that of defining a rule found in the grammars of children between 1.5 and 2.5 years. That it does not hold for adult language can be seen from sentences like

(96) a. Harry likes vodka, Fred says.
b. All hands were lost, it was feared.

in which it is the first clause which is subordinate (i.e., the complement clause), even though it has no subordination marker attached to it. More seriously, I question the supposition in the quote from Langacker that the 'natural' assumption is that the initial clause is the main clause unless otherwise marked; sentences like (96a, b) are not difficult to process and thus are not 'unnatural' in this sense (the meaning of 'natural' in the quote not being clear in any case). Notice that Langacker's proposed 'explanation' makes crucial reference to considerations of temporal order in surface structure: the expressions 'later in the sentence', 'previous context', and 'previous clause' are quite prominent in the statement. But as (96) shows, temporal order is evidently not what is involved in determining whether complementizers may appear; what IS involved is considerably more subtle and abstract.

Let us at this point reconsider briefly an issue raised in|§2.2.5 but left unresolved at that point. The question concerned whether, in situations where it was possible to avoid having C-rules for both Subjects and Objects, Subjects rather than Objects should be identified deductively. A decision was taken, arbitrarily, to identify the former deductively and the latter by C-rule, a decision that was subsequently modified so as to reverse the status of Subject and Object in passive constructions. The notion of marked vs. unmarked arguments was introduced as a means of providing rubrics for active Object/passive Subject and active Subject/ passive Object respectively. Finally, in the present chapter, two C-rules, the OR and ODC, were modified so as to make reference not to entire arguments but rather to argument segments, the constitution of whole arguments (maximal segments) then being determined on the basis of such principles as the Absolute Priority Constraint and the Second Maximization Principle.

Bearing the foregoing in mind, suppose we now consider the mechanisms provided in CORG for determining under what conditions one predicate or predication is subordinate to another. There are in fact two such mechanisms, one based on argument segment status, the other based on complementizer marking. Consider now the following fact: Either mechanism may be employed in cases of marked argument complementation — e.g., in cases like

(97) Harry knows (that) Fred likes vodka.

it is possible to rely either on the complementizer (if present) or on the segment status marking imposed by the OR to determine that *like* is associated with a subordinate predication. In cases of unmarked argument complementation, however, the segment status marking mechanism is unavailable in principle given the assumption that Subject segments in actives or Object segments in passives are not identified as such by C-rule. Thus, in

(98) That Fred likes vodka annoys Harry.

the *that*-complementizer provides literally the only available cue as to the subordinate status of *like*.

Drawing all of these considerations together, we emerge with the following picture: If marked argument complements occur without complementizers, their identifiability as such is none the less not affected, since the alternative mechanism of identification based on prior segment status marking is available. Consequently, complementizers, though permissible in marked argument complements, are redundant therein. But unmarked argument complements can be identified as such only if some overt morphological cue such as the presence of a complementizer is available; since there are no C-rules for unmarked argument segment identification, there is never any prior marking as to segment status associated with the elements of unmarked argument complements. It is thus anything but surprising that the particular asymmetry between unmarked and marked argument complements observed in English should obtain in its existing form. Notice finally that for this account to be maintained, it is crucial that we adhere to the assumptions about the relationship between unmarked and marked arguments presented in the previous chapter — that in situations where one is identified by rule and the other deductively, the former type of identification is associated with marked arguments (active Objects, passive Subjects) while the latter is associated with unmarked arguments (active Subjects, passive Objects). If we did not make these assumptions, then we would expect exactly the opposite of the existing situation with regard to complementizer marking to obtain. We may thus take the facts in this regard as evidence in favor of the particular decision adopted; some additional evidence of a related sort will be presented in the next chapter.

If the foregoing is correct, then linear order is not what is relevant to whether or not complementizer marking is required.

In a sentence such as

(99) *Harry likes vodka,* Fred says. (=(96a))

the italic segment is an Object complement of an active verb and thus does not require complementizer marking. The analysis of (99) proceeds as follows: If the ODC is to be satisfied, then *Fred* will have to be SUBJ*(say)*; by the Left Priority Constraint, *vodka* will be OBJ*(like)*, leaving *Harry* to be analyzed as SUBJ*(like)*:

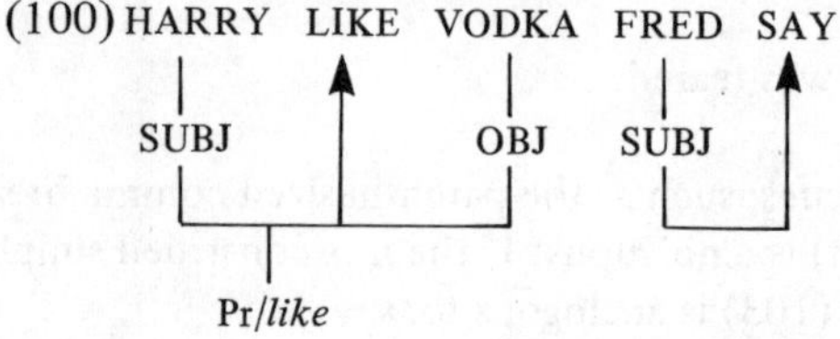

Then, by the Second Maximization Principle, Pr/*like* is OBJ*(say)* and

the final analysis is

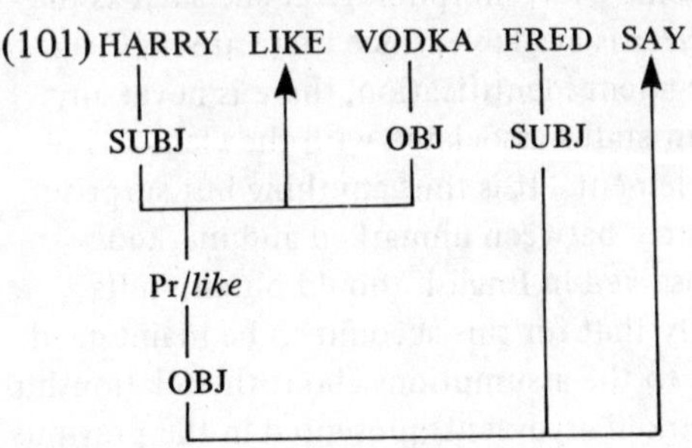

It is thus possible to determine that Pr/*like* is OBJ*(say)* without complementizers having to be taken into account.

The case of a sentence such as (96b), repeated as

(102) All hands were lost, it was feared.

is somewhat different. Here we have an instance of an unmarked
argument complement occurring without a complementizer, seemingly
in violation of our expectations. Recall, however, that our hypothesis
does not say specifically that unmarked argument complements must
have complementizers; it says only that there must be some overt
morphological cue contributing to their identification as such. I suggest
that in a sentence such as (102) the expletive *it* is the cue in question:
Whereas complementizers are subordination markers, the expletive *it*
in an extraposed construction may be viewed as a SUPERORDINATION
marker indicating that the predicate with which it is associated takes a
complement in the Subject or Object relation depending on whether
the predicate in question is active or passive. In a sentence such as
(102) the presence of the *it* is thus sufficient to establish that *all hands
were lost* must be taken as a subordinate predication. Perhaps a more
revealing example would be

(103) Harry knew (,) it was feared.

Without any intonational cues, such as the parenthesized comma break,
the string of words in (103) is ambiguous: If the *it* is construed simply
as a deictic pronoun, then (103) is analogous to, say,

(104) Harry knew the monster was feared.

where Pr/*fear* is OBJ*(know)*. On the other hand, if the *it* is construed as
a superordination marker, then Pr/*know*, however constituted, must be
subordinate to Pr/*fear*. An analysis consistent with this construal is

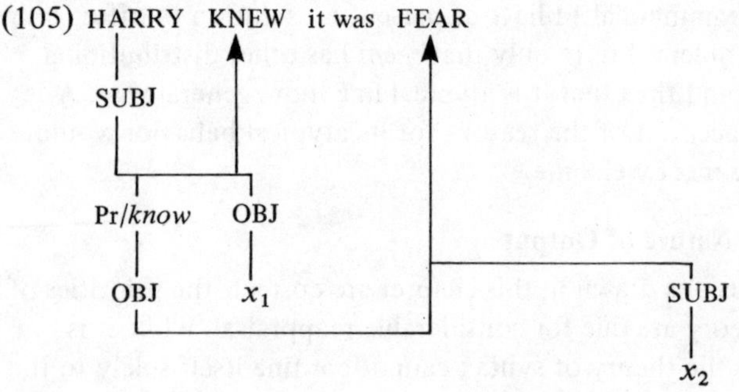

corresponding to the interpretation of (103) as a paraphrase of

(106) It was feared (by x_2) that Harry knew $|(x_1)$.

The comma break may be regarded as indicating that what precedes it
is to be construed as a predication; it does not, however, give any
indication of itself that what precedes is to be taken as subordinate
to what follows, since if that were the case, it ought to be possible to
have sentences such as

(107) *Harry knew, it was feared.

That (107) is ill-formed suggests that the identification of *Harry knew*
as an unmarked argument complement requires the presence of some
additional element — either a complementizer or a superordination
marker; the comma break alone cannot be viewed as having the function
of such elements.

Note must be taken, however, of one peculiar phenomenon which
is not consistent with our hypothesis, namely, the behavior of the
verb *seem*. Compare

(108) a. It seems (that) Harry likes vodka.
      b. Seems Harry likes vodka.
      c. *Harry likes vodka, seems.

Sentences like (108b) without the expletive *it,* often occur in colloquial

English; that this sentence is entirely well-formed even though *seem* takes an unmarked argument complement is a peculiar fact given the proposal advanced above. (That (108c) is ill-formed is, however, not particularly surprising given that even *That Harry likes vodka seems* is ungrammatical.) I have at present no solution to offer to this particular problem. I note only that *seem* has other distributional peculiarities and thus that it is atypical in a more general way. A satisfactory account of the reasons for its atypical behavior would, of course, be most welcome.

3.3. On the Nature of Output

If the conclusions drawn in this chapter are correct, the priorities of syntactic theory are due for considerable reappraisal. While it is obvious that the theory of syntax cannot confine itself solely to the description of surface structure, it appears none the less that surface structure must be given a considerably more prominent position than it has occupied in transformationally based investigations. Whereas TG has placed primary emphasis on the form of underlying structures and the rules required to map these onto surface structures, CORG focuses instead on the organization of surface structure itself in the light of the kinds of information that are to be encoded therein. The two foci are related, but they are not identical — as I hope the preceding discussion has shown. In particular, transformational theory has tended to obscure the significance of the domain problem, which, I contend, is at the very heart of the matter with which syntactic theory must come to grips in so far as it is concerned with complex sentences.

It should be pointed out, however, that there is nothing inherently revolutionary about the particular methods adopted in achieving the goals I have set here. The procedure is the time-honored one of first developing an account that will deal adequately with the simplest cases (i.e., sentences with only one predicate) and then seeking the means by which to reduce the more complex cases to instances of the simpler ones. We have found that within the domains of a complex sentence, the behavior of elements is quite similar to that of elements of simplex sentences; thus, in approaching the syntax of complex sentences, the goal is to find some means of parceling the structure in such a way as to render each parcel parallel in its structure to some simplex sentence.

This observation in turn leads us back to a point raised in Chapter 1 concerning the difference between CORG and TG. It was suggested there that the two models are not so much different hypotheses about linguistic structure as distinct metalanguages differing on a variety of points of emphasis. We suggested further that what makes one metalanguage preferable to another is the manner in which its points of emphasis lead more readily to the discovery of interesting hypotheses. Since TG places very little emphasis on the organization of surface structure (except indirectly, in so far as it is concerned with guaranteeing that a grammar has only well-formed structures as output), there is little reason for looking for such parallels as those just described between the domains of a complex sentence and simplex sentences. Since the existence of these parallels is not recognized, it comes as no surprise that such phenomena as non-normal form in complement constructions are taken as indicative of 'degeneracy' in output structures; this in turn reinforces the lack of attention paid to such structures, while favoring increased reliance on idealized hypothetical entities, which itself leads in a never-ending regression even further away from concern with the one set of objects that provide the very *raison d'être* of syntactic theory: the sentences of natural languages and what can be determined empirically about their form and content. The best way to halt this regression is to break completely with the conventional wisdom and to assume that the 'degeneracy' of surface structure is apparent rather than real. To the extent that it shows at least an inclination in this direction, recent work on 'perceptual strategies' represents one of the more promising developments of recent years; I will have more to say about this work and its relationship to the concerns of this study in Chapter 6.

Notes

1. In both analyses one NP is analyzed as an argument of two predicates — *vodka* as OBJ*(know, like)* in (5) and *Fred* as SUBJ*(like)* and OBJ*(know)* in (6); recall, however, that such analyses do not violate the Law of Uniqueness.
2. A related concern none the less does not arise pertaining to rule application; the theory of the transformational cycle, for example, seeks to limit the domain of applicability of transformations at particular points in the derivations of complex sentences.
3. This argument may be taken as merely a rewording of one of the essential items of justification for the transformational approach. Much of the thrust of transformational theory is that of compensating for what is perceived to be irregularity or degeneracy in surface structure by refusing to deal with it directly, viewing it instead as an imperfect manifestation of a hypothetical abstract level of syntactic organization with ideal structural properties. That this might be construed as an evasion of, rather than a solution to, the real problems of syntactic analysis does not seem to have been widely perceived. For further discussion of this point, see Kac 1976b.
4. See note 4 to 'Prospectus'.

4   COMPLEX SENTENCES II: NOMINAL MODIFICATION

4.1. Head-Modifier Constructions

Natural languages commonly make use of constructions of a type
traditionally characterized as consisting of two elements: a HEAD and
a MODIFIER of the head. We will henceforth refer to such constructions as HEAD-MODIFIER CONSTRUCTIONS or HMCs. In this
chapter we will be concerned with HMCs consisting of a head nominal
and a modifier in the form of a clause — e.g.,

(1)   a.   [$_H$ the claim] [$_M$ that Harry believed]
      b.   [$_H$ the claim] [$_M$ that Harry believed the allegations]

The NP in (1a) is a relative construction, that in (1b) what we might
call a COMPLEMENT NOMINAL. Both constructions may, in
accordance with current terminology, be classified as COMPLEX NPs.
It is important to note, however, that not all HMCs are NPs; because
of the phenomenon of 'extraposition from NP', a head and its modifier
may be separated — as in

(2)   a.   [$_H$ A claim] was made [$_M$ that Harry believed] .
      b.   [$_H$ A claim] was made [$_M$ that the world was flat] .

The modifier in such discontinuous HMCs will be called EXTERNAL,
as opposed to those in (1), which are INTERNAL.

In standard transformational treatments, clausal modifiers of the
kind with which we are concerned are presumed to be dominated by
S; since we have eliminated S-nodes from categorial representations,
we must devise some alternative means of analyzing such modifiers
categorially. We will henceforth assume that there is a categorial label
M such that the following rule obtains:

(3)   M ---→ X-P-Y

NOTE: An earlier version of the present chapter appears as Kac 1974a. I would
like at this early point to call the attention of the reader to a recent paper by Ray
Cattell (1976), which comes independently to conclusions not unlike those drawn
here and in the next chapter. It should also be noted that the ideas presented in
this chapter are to some extent anticipated in Grosu 1972; see the discussion in §4.6

i.e., M may dominate a sequence of elements at least one of which must be a predicate. The range of X and Y will, of course, have to be constrained in certain specific ways; the nature of at least some of the required constraints will become apparent as the chapter proceeds.

It is possible for modifiers to be PRMs — e.g., those in complement nominals. In relative constructions it is typically the entire construction which constitutes a PRM; thus (1a) manifests the predication manifested by the simplex sentence *Harry believed the claim.* An HMC, however, even though it may constitute a PRM, is something more. Its meaning is not exhausted by the content of the manifested predication. It is necessary that we have a way of distinguishing semantically between sentences such as

(4)   a. Harry knew (that) a girl liked Fred.
       b. Harry knew a girl that/who liked Fred.

In both sentences the Object of the verb includes a predication also manifested by the sentence

(5)   A girl liked Fred.

but the sentences are clearly not synonymous; for example, (4b) implies that Harry knew a girl, but (4a) does not.

We will distinguish HMCs such as that in (4b) from predicate complements like that in (4a) by introducing (or rather by taking note of) the distinction commonly made between predications and TERMS. As these notions are employed in logic, predications (or PROPOSITIONS, to use the more conventional term) denote 'states of affairs', while terms denote 'things'. If we assume that all HMCs . must be construed as terms, then we account for the 'extra' meaning properties which these elements possess above and beyond what may be conveyed by the predications they contain. Terms are presumed to be elementary arguments of predicates, thus accounting for the difference in meaning between (4a, b).

It is important that the notion 'term' not be confused with the notion 'noun phrase' or 'nominal'. Not all terms are NPs because not all terms are constituents; in (2a), for example, the discontinuous HMC *a claim . . . that Harry believed* acts as a term just as its continuous counterpart does in

(6)   A claim that Harry believed was made.

The foregoing requires a slight modification of the Law of Correspondence, which we may restate as follows:

(7)   LAW OF CORRESPONDENCE — Revised Formulation
       To every TERM in a sentence, there must correspond a statement in relational representation identifying this term as an argument of some predicate in a specified relation or marking the NP as the Object of a preposition or both.

where TERM replaces 'nonexpletive NP'. (Expletive items are thus presumed not to be terms.)

In the discussion to follow, we adopt the convention of labeling HMCs with the designation 'T' for 'term' in the diagrammatic representation of analyses. The sentences in (4) would be diagrammed as follows:

(8)   a. HARRY KNOW A GIRL LIKE FRED

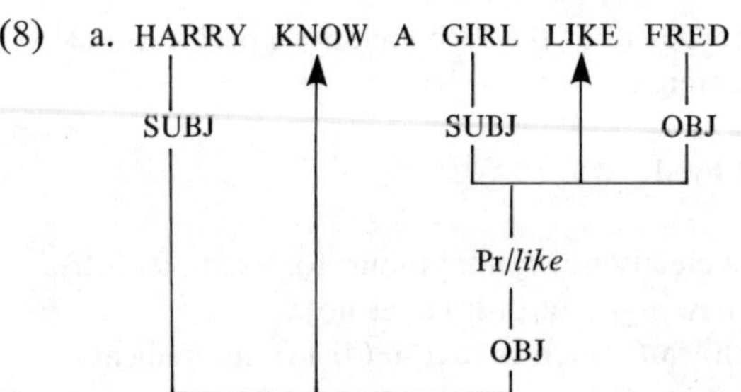

    b. HARRY KNOW A GIRL who/that LIKE FRED

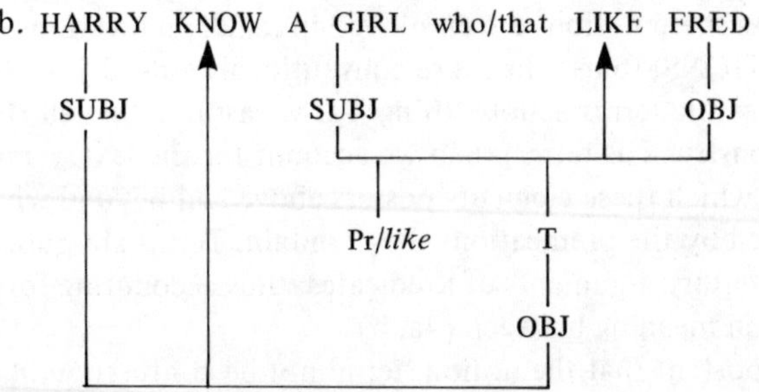

The diagram (8b) is intended to convey that the manifestation of Pr/*like* is also a term manifestation, and that it is by virtue of its term function that it is OBJ*(know)*. Notice, incidentally, that relative markers such as *who* and *that* are not considered terms in this analysis.

Complement nominals pose a special problem. In a sentence like

(9)　Harry believed *the claim that the world was flat.*

the entire complement nominal, indicated by the italics, is the Object of *believe*. The problem is this: The head NP *the claim* bears no relation to the predicate of the modifier (i.e., the adjective *flat*, whose only argument is *the world*). If it is an argument of any predicate, it must be an argument of *believe* in the relation Object; but the entire nominal has already been construed as OBJ*(believe)*. Hence we seem to be in a situation, prohibited by the metaconditions, where *the claim* must be left unanalyzed (in violation of Correspondence) or analyzed as a second Object of *believe* (in violation of Uniqueness.)

In point of fact, the second alternative can be adopted without a Uniqueness violation. In the context of a particular expression, e.g., the italic portion of (9), the head of the construction may be regarded as coreferential with the construction as a whole. Hence it is possible to impose the analysis

(10)　... BELIEVED THE CLAIM that THE WORLD BE FLAT

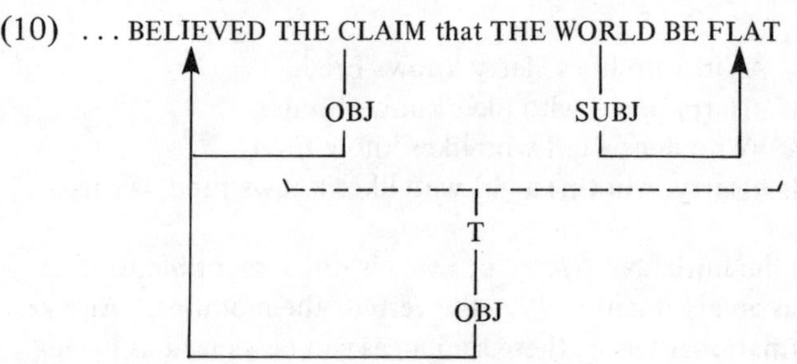

But now another problem arises, namely, that (10) might be presumed to be in violation of the Second Maximization Principle: on one interpretation of that principle, smaller elements are always supposed to be passed over for larger ones where both could be analyzed as $a(P)$ for some relation a. Such an interpretation is unwarranted, however. To say that X has priority of analyzability as $a(P)$ over Y is to say only that Y cannot be considered a candidate for $a(P)$ until X has been accounted for. If it happens that, after X has been analyzed, it remains possible to construe Y as $a(P)$ without violation of any principle of the theory, such a construal is fully permissible.

4.2.　The Complex NP Phenomenon

The central concern of this chapter is to provide at least a minimally explanatorily adequate account of the range of facts which led to the postulation, within transformational theory, of the so-called COMPLEX NP CONSTRAINT ('CNPC'); I will henceforth refer to this body of facts collectively as the 'complex NP phenomenon'.[1] Couched in the most theoretically neutral terms, a description of the phenomenon may be given as follows: despite the fact that discontinuous dependencies may hold in complex sentences across indefinitely long spans of intervening material (corresponding to what, in transformational parlance, are called ESSENTIAL VARIABLES), there are none the less particular structural configurations in which such dependencies may not hold. Thus compare

(11) a. Harry knows that Maxine likes Fred.
      b. Maxine, Harry knows likes Fred.
      c. Who does Harry know likes Fred?
      d. Maxine, who(m) Harry knows likes Fred, is smart.

with

(12) a. A girl who likes Harry knows Fred.
      b. *Harry, a girl who likes knows Fred.
      c. *Who does a girl who likes know Fred?
      d. *Harry, who(m) a girl who likes knows Fred, is smart.

In (12b-d) the initial NP *(Harry* or *who)* is not susceptible to interpretation as an argument of *like*, the verb of the modifier.[2] Analyzed in transformational terms, these sentences can be viewed as having been derived via movement operations all of which have the effect of extracting an element from a particular type of syntactic configuration, i.e.,

(13)

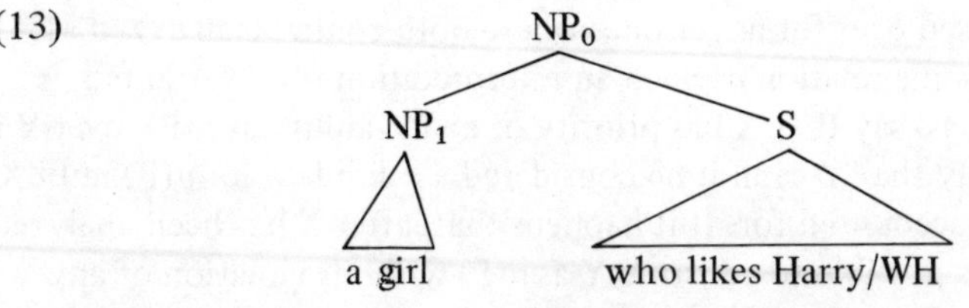

Since all the operations in question (Topicalization, Question Movement, Relative Clause Formation, etc.) would involve moving either *Harry* or WH from the S embedded in NP$_0$ outside the boundaries of NP$_0$, the proposal was made (Ross 1967) that such movements be prohibited by

the following general restriction:

(14) COMPLEX NP CONSTRAINT
No element contained in a sentence dominated by a noun
phrase with a lexical head noun may be moved out of that
noun phrase by any transformation.[3]

The term 'complex NP' in this context refers to noun phrases of the
form of NP_0 in (13). In our revised categorial scheme, (13) would
have to be re-represented as

(15)

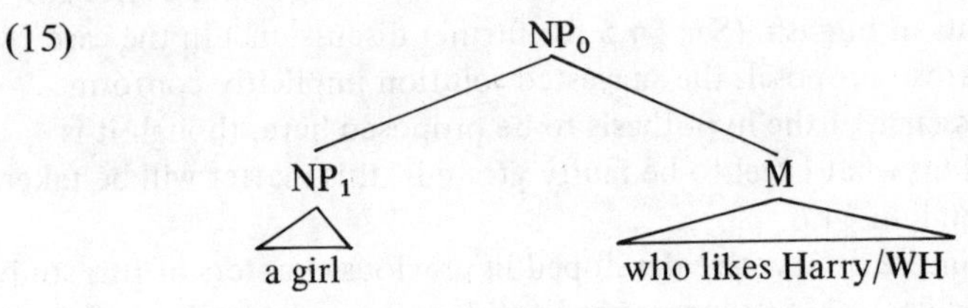

Ross's account, and the general framework within which it is
couched, is not a very satisfying one from an explanatory point of
view. While the constraint will, clearly, block a certain class of
inadmissible derivations, there is nothing in the overall theory to
indicate WHY they should be inadmissible. Indeed, the facts come
as something of a surprise, and Ross's response is simply to add an
ad hoc restriction whose function is little more than that of sealing
a leak in the overall theory. There are other reasons for dissatisfaction
as well: For one thing, the restrictions in question, however formulated,
have considerable cross-linguistic validity (if not absolute universality —
see Rodman 1973); moreover, sentences like our paradigm examples
(12b-d) are not merely ill-formed but evidently present considerable
processing difficulties — thus suggesting that what is violated in such
cases is a deep-seated restriction on the organization and presentation
of information in sentences.

In view of these considerations, we would seem well advised to
shift our viewpoint considerably. If we are to explain the complex
NP phenomenon, even at a relatively low level of explanation, we
should be looking for some general property of complex NPs,
recognition of which is required for reasons other than that of
accounting for the complex NP phenomenon but from which the
existence of the phenomenon will none the less be a consequence. One

attempt to provide such an explanation has been given by Schachter (1973) and Rodman (1973) in terms of a treatment of complex NPs as special cases of a more general class of 'foreground-background' constructions. Another, proposed by Grosu (1972), attempts an explanation in terms of perceptual considerations. I am, however, skeptical of both proposals: In the case of the Schachter-Rodman account, one problem is that the notions 'foreground' (or 'focus') and 'background' are not sufficiently well defined or intuitively accessible to be genuinely useful; moreover, as Rodman himself notes, there are counterexamples in languages such as Japanese, where the complex NP phenomenon fails to hold in anything like the strength it exhibits in English. (See §4.5 for further discussion.) In the case of the Grosu proposal, the suggested solution implicitly conforms to the essence of the hypothesis to be proposed here, though it is justified on what I feel to be faulty grounds; this matter will be taken up in detail in §4.6.

Within the perspective developed in previous chapters of this study, it is possible — at least insofar as English and typologically similar languages are concerned — to give an explanation of the complex NP phenomenon that will fulfill the minimal desiderata set above. The domain problem figures crucially in the account, in that it will turn out that the apparatus required to solve it for sentences containing HMCs accounts as well for the ill-formedness of the relevant cases. That is to say, we will explain the impossibility of (12b-d) on the grounds that, given the domain structure that must be assigned to them for independent reasons, violation of the metaconditions invariably ensues. Recall that domain restrictions are required to determine certain facts concerning WELL-FORMED sentences — this constituting the independent motivation of the apparatus to be presented. The results thus obtained, if valid, may be taken as further confirmation of a strategy based on consideration of the properties of surface structures rather than rules or derivations.

4.3. HMCs as Predicate Domains

It will be crucial for what is to follow that we have a principle for identifying the element acting as the head with regard to each modifier that occurs in a sentence. This may be done straightforwardly enough, via the following:

(16) HEAD IDENTIFICATION PRINCIPLE
      If a modifier M shares a directly dominating nominal node

NOM$_i$ with a second nominal node NOM$_j$, then NOM$_j$ is the head with respect to M; otherwise, the choice of head is free, except as restricted by other principles of the theory.

Thus, in configurations of the form

(17)

NOM$_1$ must be the head with respect to M. If the HMC is discontinuous, however, there will be no directly dominating node shared by M and any nominal, and the choice of head is not restricted. For example, in the ambiguous sentence

(18)   A man is dating my sister who owns a Maserati.

one reading coincides with the case where the relative clause is external and *a man* is chosen as head; in the other case, either the relative clause is presumed internal to the NP *my sister who owns a Maserati* or, equivalently, is presumed external, but *my sister* rather than *a man* is selected as head by the Head Identification Principle.

We now take up the matter of determining the domain structure of complex sentences containing HMCs with clausal Ms. We begin by considering relative constructions — e.g.,

(19)   A girl who likes Harry knows Fred. (=(12a))

for which the initial result will be

(20)   A GIRL who LIKE HARRY KNOW FRED

(That *Harry* must be OBJ*(like)* rather than *Fred* follows from the Left Priority Constraint.) If we assume that *a girl who likes Harry* has been categorially analyzed as an HMC, then the remainder of the analysis can be determined in straightforward fashion. Since HMCs are terms, the HMC in this case must be an argument of some predicate. If we assume, as seems reasonable, that no term can be an argument of a predicate contained within it, then the HMC in (19) can only be an argument of *know.* This leaves *a girl* unanalyzed, but *like* still requires a Subject; thus, the final analysis is

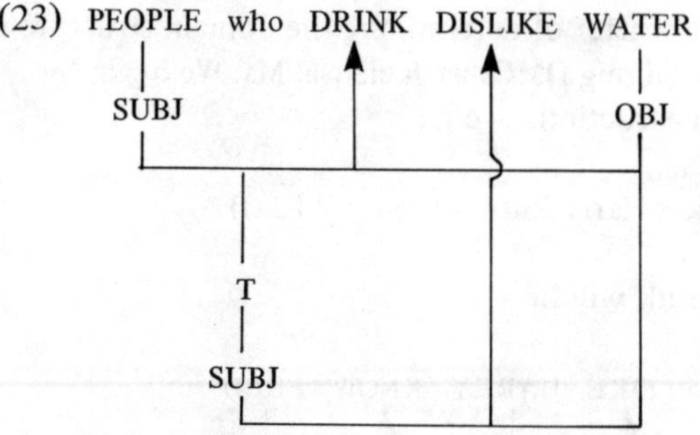

There are, however, situations which are not so straightforward. Thus, consider

(22) People who drink dislike water.

Given the principles developed so far, the following ought to be a possible analysis of (22):

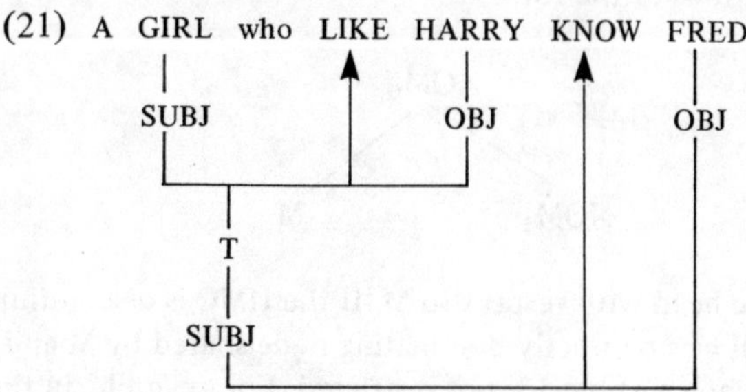

But this is impossible; most specifically, *water* cannot actually be read as an Object of *drink* in the sentence in question; rather, the only correct analysis of (22) must be

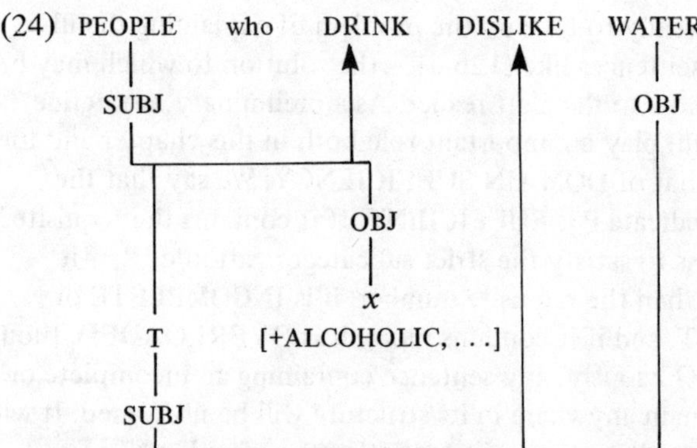

A result like (23) will be blocked if we adopt the following restriction:

(25) HMC DOMAIN RESTRICTION (HDR)
No element outside the M constituent of an HMC other than
the head with respect to this M is eligible for analysis as an
argument of a predicate contained in the M.

The effect of the HDR will be to rule out analyses such as (23), since
water is outside the HMC and is not the head of the HMC. Note,
incidentally, that this presupposes a further restriction to the effect
that a modifier can have no more than one head defined in relation
to it.

Now compare (22) and

(26) *People who like drink water.

This sentence has the same superficial form as (22); however, the
predicate *like,* unlike *drink*, is surface-transitive — i.e., it must occur
in surface structure with an overt Object. The HDR correctly predicts
that (26) will be ill-formed, since, if *water* is eliminated from the range
of terms that can be Objects of *drink*, its strict subcategorization
cannot be satisfied. We thus capture the fact that (26) is ill-formed
for the same reason as

(27) *People like.

even though in (26) an element susceptible to analysis as OBJ*(like)*
occurs in the sentence.

We are now ready to take up the problem of explaining the ill-formedness of sentences like (12b-d) — the solution to which may be apparent even now to the alert reader. As a preliminary, we define a notion that will play an important role both in this chapter and the next, namely, that of DOMAIN SUFFICIENCY. We say that the domain of a predicate P is SUFFICIENT iff it contains the requisite number of terms to satisfy the strict subcategorization of P; if it contains fewer than the requisite number, it is INCOMPLETE or INSUFFICIENT, and if it contains more, it is OVERLOADED, though still sufficient. Obviously, any sentence containing an incomplete or overloaded domain anywhere in its structure will be ill-formed. It will be our claim that all sentences instantiating the complex NP phenomenon will be seen to involve either incompleteness or over-loading or both in some domain or domains.

Let us now repeat our original examples from (12):

(28)   a.   *Harry, a girl who likes knows Fred. (=(12b))
       b.   *Who does a girl who likes know Fred? (=(12c))
       c.   *Harry, who(m) a girl who likes knows Fred is smart. (=(12d))

Take (28b) as a paradigm case. The categorial structure of this sentence is as follows:

(29)

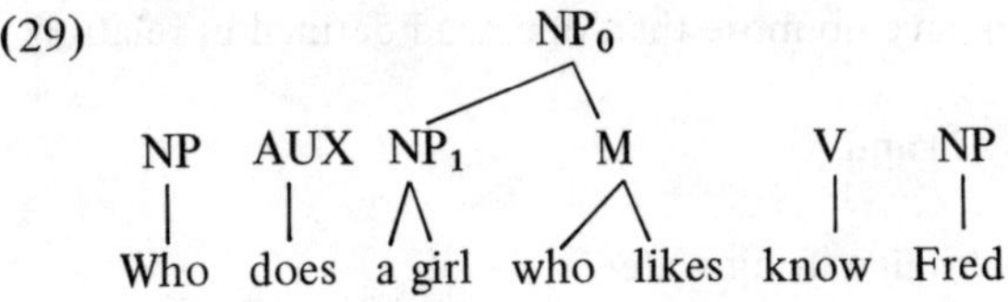

Given the HDR, it is predicted that this sentence will be ill-formed, since (a) NP_0 will constitute an incomplete domain (i.e., D/*like*), while (b) D/*know* will be overloaded. The first point follows from the fact that no element outside NP_0, the HMC, can be taken as an argument of *like*; since NP_0 contains only one term, however, the strict subcategorization of the predicate will be incapable of satisfaction. The second point holds for essentially the same reason. NP_0 will have to be an argument of *know*, as will *Fred*; this leaves *who* to be accounted for. The strict subcategorization is already satisfied by the terms NP_0 and *Fred*, neither of which is either coreferential or coordinate with *who*. But *who*, by the HDR, cannot be an argument of *like* and thus could only be construed as an argument of *know*. But then the domain of *know* is overloaded, since Correspondence and Uniqueness cannot be simultaneously satisfied within this domain. D/*know* contains too many terms as a consequence of the terms being wrongly distributed in the structure.

Let us now consider a case involving a complement nominal:

(30) *Who did the claim that Harry liked bother Maxine?

for which the categorial representation is

(31)

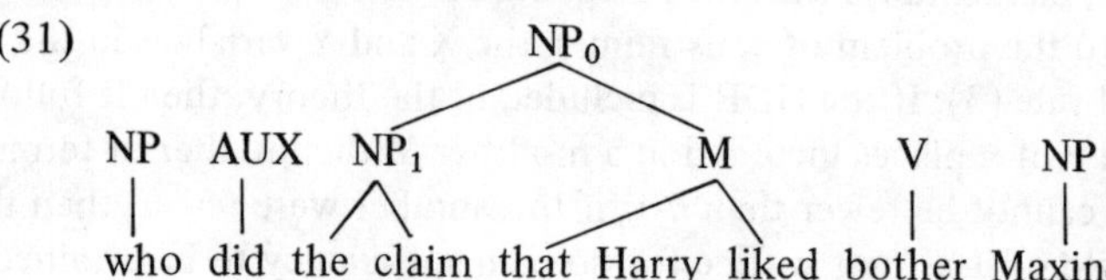

In this case, the HMC need not necessarily be regarded as incomplete; *the claim that Harry liked* can stand on its own as a sufficient domain (though it would not be interpretable as a complement nominal). But the remaining domain, D/*bother,* is overloaded even so. NP_0 and *Maxine* must both be arguments of *bother*, thus rendering the domain sufficient. As before, however, *who* will be incapable of being taken as an argument either of *like* (by the HDR) or of *bother* (by Uniqueness-b). Thus (30) must also be ill-formed.

The examples considered thus far involve continuous HMCs. Let us now consider a case with a discontinuous construction:

(32) *What did a boy come in who was drinking?

Such cases are of special relevance in the context of a comparison of CORG and TG, since one of the arguments for the necessity of a movement transformation of Extraposition from NP involves precisely the fact that without such a transformation the ill-formedness of (32) cannot be accounted for by the CNPC. One important difference between the two approaches, however, is that the relevant constraint in CORG is defined on a more general class of constructions than complex NPs — i.e., on the class of HMCs in general. With respect to (32), we proceed as follows: By the Head Identification Principle, either *what* or *a boy* could be picked as the head relative to the modifier *who was drinking.* That both cannot be picked follows from the assumption stated previously that a given modifier may have only one head defined relative to it. But then, (32) contains an overloaded domain, since regardless of what choice is made in determining the head with respect to the relative clause, the HMC so constructed must be an argument of *come* by virtue of being a term. This leaves the NP not selected as head incapable of being analyzed as an argument of any predicate, since it cannot be in relation with the predicate of the modifier and cannot be an argument of *come* without a Uniqueness violation ensuing. Thus, the situation in the case of (32) is exactly comparable to those involving continuous HMCs.

Notice, incidentally, that the foregoing account also gives a partial solution to the problem of constraining the X and Y variables in the categorial rule (3). If the HDR is included in the theory, then it follows that for a P of n-places included in a modifier M the number of terms within M cannot be fewer than n-1; if the number were fewer, then the head would of itself not suffice for domain sufficiency to be attained, and the HMC as a whole would be incomplete.

The foregoing illustrates the manner in which the complex NP phenomenon is to be accounted for within a CORG framework. The crucial point to bear in mind is that the facts pertaining to the phenomenon are consequences of the HDR, this constraint being independently motivated in that its original purpose was to solve the domain problem for well-formed sentences such as (22). Moreover, ill-formed sentences such as (26) are ruled out by the HDR, whereas the CNPC is of no relevance to such cases. But it is certainly no coincidence that (26) and, say,

(33)   *Whiskey, people who like drink water.

are both ill-formed, since both contain the HMC *people who like*. The HDR, in other words, acts as exactly the condition on the organization and presentation of information in sentences that, as we suggested above, must be responsible for the facts in question.

4.4. A Further Phenomenon

At this point, I introduce some new data which suggest that the complex NP phenomenon is somewhat more subtle than has previously been recognized. As an approach to the issue at hand, I present first the results of an informal informant survey carried out with sentences of the type we may have been treating in this chapter. The survey was in two parts, the first of which called for judgements about individual sentences, while the second called for judgements in which sentences were compared with each other. The sentences used are enumerated below:

(34) a. Harry knows a girl who likes Fred.
      b. A girl who likes Fred knows Harry.
      c. Fred, Harry knows a girl who likes. (M)
      d. It's Fred that Harry knows a girl who likes. (M)
      e. Fred, a girl who likes knows Harry. (U)
      f. It's Fred that a girl who likes knows Harry. (U)
      g. Who does a girl who likes know Harry? (U)
      h. Who does Harry know a girl who likes? (M)
      i. Fred, whom Harry knows a girl who likes, is smart. (M)
      j. Fred, whom a girl who likes knows Harry, is smart. (U)

The letters 'M' and 'U' indicate the sentences that have incomplete marked and unmarked arguments respectively.

The subjects in the survey were students in an introductory syntax course at the University of Minnesota — thirty-one in all. All had a slight acquaintance with the Complex NP Constraint, which had been mentioned in passing several times but to which no careful attention had been paid up to that point. No students in the class had any acquaintance with corepresentational grammar.

For the first part of the survey, the subjects were presented with the list of sentences shown in (34) and asked to judge for each sentence whether it was 'easy, difficult, or impossible to understand'. Use of the terms 'grammatical/ungrammatical' was avoided; all judgements were to be made with reference to intelligibility.

The results of the first part of the survey are summarized in Table 1. The first three columns show, for each sentence, the number of 'easy' (E), 'difficult' (D), and 'impossible' (I) judgements delivered. The fourth column shows how many subjects made judgements other than 'easy' (D/I). Finally, the fifth column gives an 'intelligibility index' (IX) determined as follows: The number of E judgements for each sentence was multiplied by 3, the number of D judgements by 2, and the number of I judgements by 1. The three products for each sentence were then totalled to yield IX. As the table shows, all of the sentences with incomplete complex NPs, whether in marked or unmarked argument position, were treated as posing significant processing difficulties. This is, of course, precisely the expected result. But the second part of the survey reveals something not shown in the figures in the table; in this part, the subjects were presented with pairs of sentences on which judgement had already been passed, shown in (35).

Table 1: Results of Informant Survey (Part I)

Sentence	E	D	I	D/I	IX
a.	31	0	0	0	93
b.	31	0	0	0	93
c. M	1	16	14	30	49
d. M	1	13	17	30	46
e. U	11	14	16	30	47
f. U	0	16	15	31	47
g. U	0	5	26	31	36
h. M	1	5	25	30	38
i. M	1	20	10	30	53
j. U	0	10	21	31	41

(35) a. Fred, Harry knows a girl who likes. (=(34c)) M
    b. Fred, a girl who likes knows Harry. (=(34e)) U
    c. Who does a girl who likes know Harry? (=(34g)) U
    d. Who does Harry know a girl who likes? (=(39h)) M
    e. Fred, whom a girl who likes knows Harry, is smart. (=(34j)) U
    f. Fred, whom Harry knows a girl who likes, is smart. (=(34i)) M
    g. It's Fred that a girl who likes knows Harry. (=(34f)) U
    h. It's Fred that Harry knows a girl who likes. (=(34d)) M

The subjects were instructed to select for each pair the member that was 'easier to understand'. Table 2 summarizes the results:

Table 2: Results of Informant Survey (Part II)

Sentence	Number of Subjects Making 'Easier' Judgement
a. M	20
b. U	10
c. U	8
d. M	22
e. U	6
f. M	24
g. U	10
h. M	20

(One subject did not respond to this section.) What is interesting here is that the M-member of each pair was rated easier by a majority of subjects in a ratio of at least 2 to 1. This in turn suggests that the M and U cases are not exactly equivalent and that the former may be expected in general to pose fewer processing difficulties than the latter. How is this asymmetry, which we will call the 'M-U asymmetry', to be explained? A tentative hypothesis might be developed along the following lines:

We begin by laying down some assumptions which must be granted if the hypothesis is to be presumed valid. These assumptions appear plausible, though of course the possibility is always open that further evidence might eventually call them into question. They are as follows:

(a) Every sentence with more than one predicate must have a domain structure imposed upon it by some principle or principles.

(b) Some sentences may be of an indeterminate status in that they are subject to the assignment of more than one kind of domain structure, that is, more than one kind of principle may be relevant to such sentences, and the results of applying them may differ.

(c) Where the situation described in (b) obtains, if the kinds of domain structure assigned lead to conflicting results with regard to well-formedness, the sentence in question will be of an ambivalent status — not entirely well-formed but of a higher degree of acceptability than a sentence for which no relevant principles predict well-formedness.

In the light of these assumptions, let us examine a typical M-case, e.g.

(36)   Fred, Harry knows a girl who likes.

This sentence is of the kind of indeterminate status described in (b). On the one hand, if its domain structure is assigned via the HDR, the sentence contains both an incomplete and an overloaded domain and thus is predicted to be ill-formed. But there is a SECOND way of assigning domain structure to (36), with different results — namely, the segment status principles of Chapter 3. If these principles are used as the basis for determining the domain structure of the sentence, it is predicted to be well-formed under the analysis

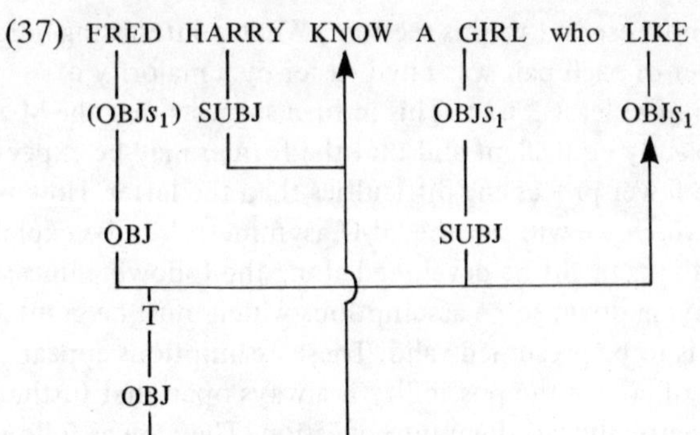

In other words, (37) could be viewed as analogous to, say,

(38) Fred, Harry knows (that) a girl likes.

The U-case corresponding to (36) is

(39) Fred, a girl who likes knows Harry.

In such a situation the segment status marking method is inapplicable in principle; thus (39) can be assigned a domain structure only by the HDR.

Now, if the assumption (c) is granted, then it is predicted that (36) should be more acceptable than (39). If the data in Table 2 are reliable, then the preponderant majority of speakers behave consistently with this prediction. The M-U asymmetry is thus explainable once it is noted that the M cases meet the conditions described in assumption (b), while the U cases do not. We will therefore take assumption (c) as a tentative hypothesis for the explanation of the facts involved.

Notice that if the M-U asymmetry is validly explained in this way, further support is given to our original decision to identify marked arguments by C-rule and unmarked arguments by deduction in situations where one type of argument is identifiable in one of these two ways and the other type is identifiable in the other. There is, in fact, a strong parallel between the explanation of the M-U asymmetry in sentences containing incomplete HMCs and the proposed explanation of the asymmetry between marked and unmarked argument complements with respect to the obligatoriness of complementizer marking.

4.5. Some Cross-Linguistic Observations

I would now like to consider some facts from languages other than
English which provide additional support for the approach to the complex NP phenomenon developed in this chapter. Specifically, I will
discuss the syntactic properties of two languages which have been
problematic when viewed in the light of earlier approaches to the complex NP phenomenon: Thai and Japanese. In brief, the problems for
these two languages are as follows:

In Thai, as in English, it is impossible to have discontinuous
dependencies of the type that would obtain if sentences like (12b-d)
were well-formed. But, as Rodman (1973) points out, the Thai facts
are problematical for Ross's theory, since a number of the relevant
processes are not naturally describable in terms of movement transformations. For example, relative clauses in Thai, if analyzed transformationally, are formed not by a two-step process of pronominalization
and movement but by deletion of a nominal from the embedded clause
under identity to the head of the HMC. The following example
illustrates:

(40)   phǒm chô:b [$_{NP}$ khru: [$_S$ thî dỳ:m nom kâe:w ní]]|

    I   like   teacher   COMP drink milk glass this
    'I like the teacher who drank this glass of milk.'

where COMP is a marker indicating that an embedded clause follows.
The derivation of the relative construction in (40) is diagrammed
below:

(41) a.

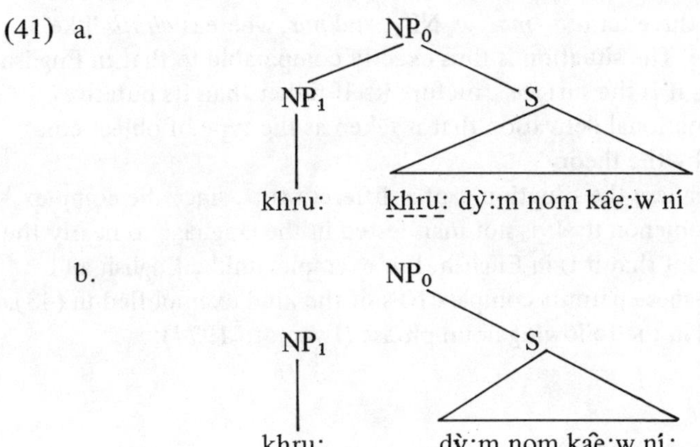

b.

where the underscore in (41a) indicates the deleted element.

The problem is this:. In Thai, as in English, relativization is impossible in constructions like (12d). Thus the following sentence is ill-formed in Thai just as its counterpart in English is:

(42)   *mae:w thî : phû cha:j thî: hĕn chɔ̂:b mǎ: tua nán dam
         cat   COMP   man   COMP see like dog CL that black
    ‘*The cat that the man who saw likes that dog is black.’

where CL is a 'classifier' associated with *nán* 'that'. But if relative clauses are formed in a transformational analysis by deletion rather than by movement, the CNPC cannot account for the ill-formedness of (42).

In a corepresentational treatment, however, the English and Thai facts are susceptible to a uniform treatment. The form of the complex NP in (42) is

(43)

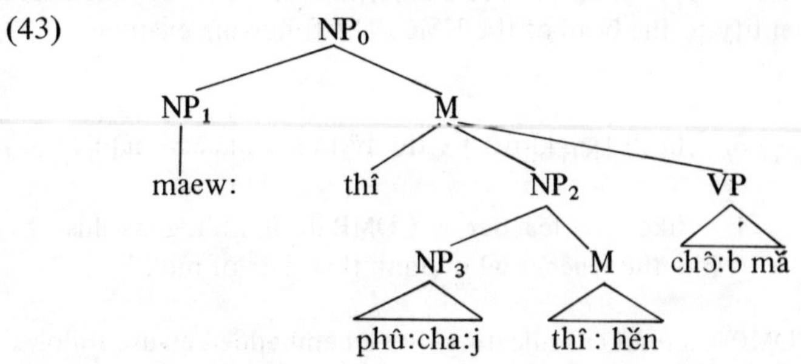

The embedded complex NP, NP_2, is — like its English translation *the man who saw* — incomplete. Moreover, NP_0 is overloaded, since it contains three terms — *mae:w*, NP_2, and *mǎ*, whereas *chɔ̂:b* 'like' is two-place. The situation is thus exactly comparable to that in English, as long as it is the surface structure itself rather than its putative transformational derivation that is taken as the type of object constrained by the theory.

In Japanese the situation is of a different sort, since the complex NP phenomenon itself is not manifested in the language to nearly the same extent that it is in English. For example, unlike English and Thai, Japanese permits complex NPs of the kind exemplified in (43), as shown in the following noun phrase (Iwamoto 1974):

(44)   osieta seito ga rakudaisita sensei
       taught student Subj. marker flunked professor
       '*the professor who the student that taught flunked.'

The structure of (44) may be given as follows:

(45)

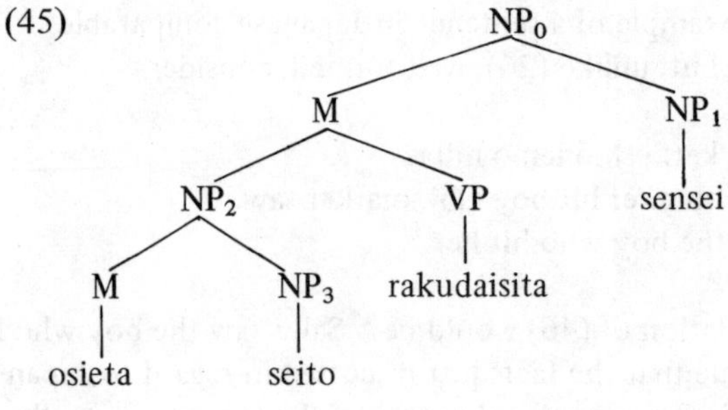

(For comparable examples involving other types of constructions in Japanese, see Rodman 1973.)

Japanese is problematical for either theory in so far as the relevant constraints are proposed as universals. Indeed, the Japanese facts show that the relevant constraints CANNOT be considered universal. But the natural question to ask at this point is why Japanese should behave as it does. Within the context of a corepresentational approach, I believe an answer can be given. If the approach is correct, then even though a language might not obey the HDR, we would expect certain other features of its syntax to vary accordingly. To make this some-what clearer, let us consider just what the HDR does in the grammar of English. Recall that the interest of this constraint lies in the fact that not only does it rule out a certain class of ill-formed constructions, but it accounts as well for certain semantic properties of well-formed sentences; in addition, it correctly predicts ill-formedness for another class of constructions (illustrated by (26)) for which the CNPC provides no account. Now, if Japanese allows constructions such as (45), what we would then be led to expect is that its general domain structure differs from that of English or Thai; specifically, we would expect to find well-formed constructions in Japanese comparable to (26), constructions which are well-formed because Japanese — for some reason — permits elements other than the head of an HMC to be in relation with the predicate of the modifier. This expectation is fulfilled and for a natural reason: unlike English (or Thai), Japanese has 'zero pronouns'. Thus, in constructions where English or Thai would require the presence of anaphoric pronouns related to specific antecedents, Japanese can simply leave the pronominal position empty. Given that the language allows for such a possibility, any 'incomplete' HMC is always subject to a construal such that it is analyzed as containing a zero pronoun whose antecedent may be outside the HMC itself. In such circumstances, searches outside HMCs must be permitted.[4] As an example of a sentence in Japanese comparable structurally to (26) but, unlike (26), well-formed, consider

(46)   Sally wa o ketta shiōnen o mita.
       Sally Subj. marker hit boy Obj. marker saw.
       'Sally saw the boy who hit her.'

A more literal translation of (46) would be '*Sally saw the boy who hit.' I would thus argue that the facts just discussed in regard to Japanese show that the seemingly exceptional nature of the language actually gives support to the overall view being taken in this chapter. It is a consequence of the underlying assumptions of this approach that if structures of the type exemplified in (45) are well-formed that certain other structures — like those exemplified in (46) — should be well-formed also. That this expectation is borne out thus constitutes evidence in favor of the corepresentational approach.

4.6. The Perceptual Conflict Hypothesis: A Critique

I conclude this chapter by commenting briefly on the account of the complex NP phenomenon recently proposed by Grosu (1972), which has certain properties in common with that advanced here. Implicitly, at least, Grosu seems to assume a principle very much like the HDR, though it is couched in different terms and has an entirely different rationale; it is the rationale that I want to subject to scrutiny here.

Grosu's argument, in brief, is that sentences instantiating the complex NP phenomenon present the hearer with a type of structural arrangement that leads to 'perceptual conflict' in processing, i.e., that some element must be perceived as having simultaneously two disparate and incompatible values along a single parameter. He develops this argument as follows: Complex NPs are treated as instances of a general type of construction which Grosu calls the NUCLEUS-AND-SATELLITE or 'N&S' construction. The term 'nucleus' is essentially synonymous with 'head' and 'satellite' with 'optional dependent of a nucleus' (though Grosu does not define the term 'dependent' explicitly). The nucleus constituent of an N&S is defined as obligatory and self-sufficient, while the satellite constituent is optional and non-self-sufficient. Grosu further assumes that by virtue of its self-sufficient status, the nucleus ranks higher on a scale of 'primacy' than the satellite within the N&S and that this therefore entails that the satellite 'depends' exclusively on the nucleus of the N&S within which it occurs. Thus, in reconstructing 'missing' material from the satellite (e.g., in the case of a relative clause, in which one argument of the predicate is typically not present), only the nucleus can be taken into account in determining the content of this material. A sentence manifesting the complex NP phenomenon is taken to contain a 'discontinuous satellite', i.e., to be analyzed as follows:

(47) $[_{SAT_1}$ Fred] $[_{N\&S} [_{NUC}$ a girl] $[_{SAT_2}$ who likes]] knows Harry.

The source of the perceptual conflict is then claimed to be the following: SAT_2 must be perceived as simultaneously exclusively dependent on the nucleus and yet not exclusively dependent on it (since SAT_1 must also be taken into account if a 'complete' satellite is to be reconstructed). (The requirement that satellites be exclusively dependent on the nuclei with which they are associated is what is comparable to the HDR in our approach.)

Couched in such terms, there are two things that are wrong with this proposal. The first is that the sense in which 'perceptual conflict' is involved here is vacuous; the ill-formedness of a sentence like (47) is not a consequence of any independent psychological principle but of properties imputed to the N&S construction itself. If it is granted that the nucleus has primacy over the satellite and that this entails exclusive dependence of the latter on the former, then the only sense in which (47) presents a conflict is the sense in which ALL ill-formed sentences present a conflict: if some operation is prohibited by some principle (or if some structural arrangement is prohibited), then carrying out the operation or generating the structural arrangement is in conflict with the prohibition against doing so. In other words, 'perceptual conflict' is, in this instance, merely a different locution for 'violation of a constraint' and hence serves no explanatory purpose.

The second problem concerns the notion 'N&S construction' itself. If perceptual conflict is not the basis for the explanation, then the issue boils down to whether recourse to the notion of the N&S construction type has an explanatory utility in itself. Here, too, I find that the answer must be negative, since Grosu's development of the notion is not sufficiently rigorous. Everything hinges crucially on two claims: first, that the nucleus ranks higher on a scale of primacy than the satellite and second, that this entails that the satellite should depend exclusively on the nucleus. The problem is that 'primacy' is not defined by Grosu, so that we have no way of knowing if the first claim is correct.[5] Moreover, there is also no way, if 'primacy over Y' entails 'Y is exclusively dependent on X'. Consequently, the notion 'N&S construction' is itself not sufficiently coherent to contribute to any illumination of the nature of the complex NP phenomenon.

As I have already noted, the foregoing is intended to be a critique of rationale and not of substance. Grosu's exclusive dependence principle, though conceived of within what I regard as an inadequate theoretical framework, none the less makes essentially the right claims. I would favor making such principles themselves the focus of attention, rather than such questionable notions as 'N&S construction', 'primacy', 'perceptual conflict', and so on.

My purpose in this chapter has been to justify empirically a framework which presents the complex NP in a more revealing light than that cast by the standard transformational account. I claim that the corepresentational account has greater explanatory adequacy in the sense that it links the complex NP phenomenon to the set of phenomena represented by the domain problem, thereby providing access to a set of independently motivated principles which have the complex NP phenomenon as a logical consequence. A deeper explanation may well have to be provided in psychological terms and would account for the nature of domain restrictions themselves; it would determine what could and could not be a possible domain restriction and would also perhaps relate domain restrictions to more general principles governing perception and information processing. An explanation of this sort cannot be provided, however, until it is clearly established what it is that is to be explained. If the conclusions of this chapter are correct, then this purpose at least has been accomplished.

Notes

1. In fact, the phenomenon involves more than just complex NPs, since discontinuous HMCs behave just as complex NPs do with regard to the particular restrictions that must be recognized. The term 'complex NP phenomenon' is chosen more for its mnemonic value than its accuracy.
2. An anonymous reader of an earlier version of this study reports disagreement with the generally accepted judgements as to the ill-formedness of examples commonly used to illustrate the complex NP phenomenon. An informant survey, the results of which are reported in §4.4, nonetheless confirms these judgements at least as applied to individual sentences.

Significantly, however, informants asked to COMPARE certain examples on which they had previously passed judgement showed a strong tendency to consider certain ones more acceptable than others. A hypothesis as to why this should be is presented in §4.4. My thanks to the reader for calling to my attention some interesting and, to my knowledge, hitherto unnoticed facts pertaining to the phenomenon under investigation.

3. But see Cattell 1976 for an ingenious argument to the effect that the ill-formedness of such sentences as (12b-d) cannot be accounted solely in terms of prohibited movements.

4. This points up one respect in which the HDR is too strong even for English. In a sentence like *People who like it drink vodka, vodka* is OBJ*(like)* by transmission (see §2.2.3 for discussion of this notion), given that it is analyzed as the antecedent of *it*. Thus, the HDR needs to be qualified in such a way that it does not apply where an argument of a predicate is identified as such on the basis of anaphora.

5. The term 'primacy' is due to Langacker (1969) and is intended to provide a rubric under which to subsume the relations 'commands' and 'precedes'. But Grosu evidently does not employ the term in this sense, since the 'primacy' relation that he regards as relevant is neither of the aforementioned, but rather one of 'centrality' – which he also does not define.

5 COMPLEX SENTENCES III: COORDINATE STRUCTURE

5.1. Some General Properties of Coordination

An adequate theory of coordination is of special importance in CORG since a crucial metacondition (Uniqueness-b) is dependent on the possibility of being able to determine formally when two elements are coordinate. In addition, coordinate structures, like other complex sentences, may present a domain problem. The solution to the domain problem for coordinate structures will, expectedly, explain the facts motivating the Coordinate Structure Constraint ('CSC') in transformational theory; the result is analogous to that obtained in the previous chapter with regard to the complex NP phenomenon.[1]

We will assume henceforth that any two elements of a sentence are susceptible to being construed as coordinate if a coordinating conjunction occurs between them. It is not necessary, however, that the conjunction be the only intervening element. Compare

(1)   a. Harry and Fred left.
      b. Harry left, and Fred (too).

In both sentences, *Harry* and *Fred* may be viewed as coordinate, and thus both may be analyzed as SUBJ*(leave)*.

A second condition under which two elements may be coordinate is one in which both are coordinate with some third element, though not necessarily separated by a conjunction. For example, in

(2)   Harry, Fred, and George left.

Harry and *Fred* are both coordinate with *George* by our previous assumption. By the second assumption, they may then be construed as coordinate with each other.

It is commonly assumed that putative coordinates must be elements 'of the same kind'; this supposed constraint has, however, proved resistant to a hard and fast formalization. For purposes of this chapter, it turns out that no such constraint need be imposed – that is, the problems with which we will be concerned do not require for their solution that we have a way of deciding whether or not putative coordinates are similar in particular ways. This is not to deny, however, that the problem of defining precisely the notion 'of the same kind' must be solved for various other purposes.

We will say that two coordinate elements are STRICTLY coordinate if no element other than a conjunction intervenes between them (thereby allowing for the possibility of no element at all intervening between coordinates). Thus *Harry* and *Fred* are strictly coordinate both in (1a) and in (2). If elements other than a conjunction intervene between coordinates, the coordinates are LOOSELY coordinate – e.g., *Harry* and *Fred* in (1b).

According to Uniqueness-b, if two elements are coordinate, they may be analyzed as bearing the same relation to a single predicate. There are, however, cases where elements which are coordinate by our definition cannot be so analyzed. For example, consider

(3)   Harry kissed Maxine and Fred hugged Samantha.

the correct analysis of which is

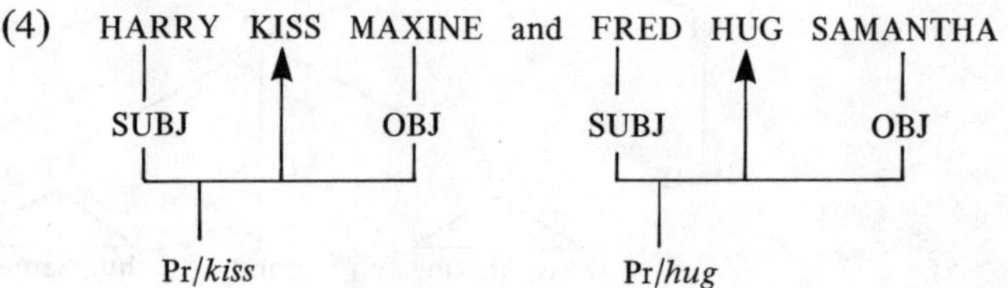

In other words, no single NP in this sentence is an argument of more than one predicate. But various pairs of NPs could by our definition be construed as coordinate; for example, *Maxine* and *Fred* could be taken as coordinate and thus ought to be analyzable as OBJ*(kiss)* or SUBJ*(hug)* or both. That such a possibility does not arise for sentences like that in question indicates that our definition of coordination must be supplemented by domain restrictions. Before describing in detail the domain restrictions required for coordinate structure, let us first eliminate the possibility that they can be naturally formulated with respect to constituent structure. To deal with a case like (3), it would seem natural enough to simply state that the domain of each predicate is confined to its own S. Recall, however, that we have eliminated S-nodes from categorial structure; moreover, it can be shown that the putative constraint just described will fail in any case. In a sentence like

(5)   Harry kissed Maxine and hugged Samantha.

for which we may give the analysis

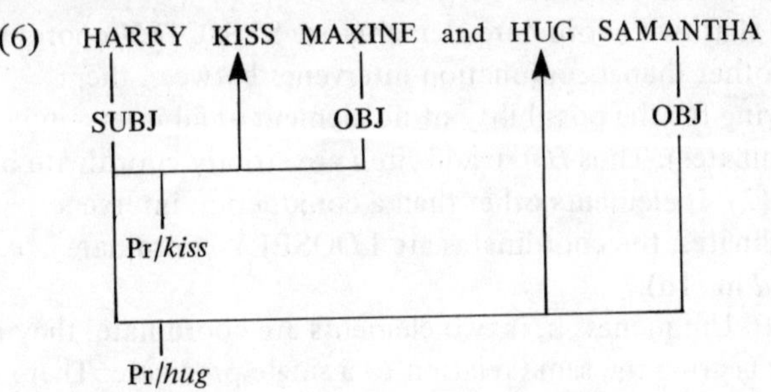

the two Object NPs are each in relation with only one predicate, whereas the Subject NP is in relation with both. Given the standard assumptions, (5) would have the constituent structure analysis

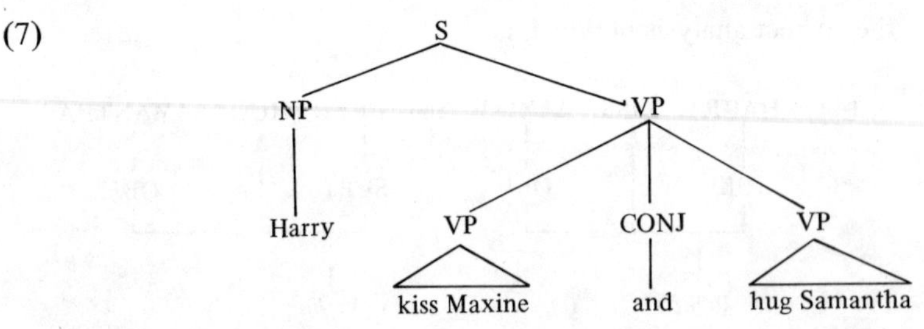

in which there is only one S-node. Since the *kiss* and *hug* domains are partially restricted, there must be some domain division imposed on the sentence independently of the presence or absence of S-nodes. However this division is accomplished, morover, it must account for the fact that *Harry* is in the domain of both verbs, whereas this is untrue of either of the other two NPs in the sentence.

There exists a way of defining domain structure on coordinate sentences which will handle cases like (3) and (5) and others as well in a uniform manner. To state the restrictions involved, we must first introduce a further notion, that of what we will call PARALLEL coordination. A coordinate structure is an instance of parallel coordination iff it has an exhaustive division into segments such that each of the following conditions is met:

(8)   a. Each segment contains a predicate and at least one
           potential argument thereof;

   b. The segments exhibit the same degree of domain sufficiency;
   c. The segments are strictly coordinate.

We will refer to such segments as p-SEGMENTS, and a division of a coordinate structure into p-segments will be called a PARALLEL SEGMENTATION. We now posit the following:

(9)   COORDINATE STRUCTURE DOMAIN CONSTRAINT (CSDC)
No element within a p-segment may function as an argument of a predicate in any other p-segment.

Returning now to (3), we observe that it is subject to the following parallel segmentation:

(10) Harry kissed Maxine and Fred hugged Samantha

$$p_1 \qquad\qquad\qquad p_2$$

Each of the conditions in (8) is satisfied by this division: both segments contain a predicate and at least one potential argument thereof; both exhibit the same degree of domain sufficiency (both are complete); and the segments are strictly coordinate. Under such a segmentation, then, given the CSDC, the analysis (4) is correctly assigned. Now consider sentence (5), here repeated as

(11) Harry kissed Maxine and hugged Samantha.

Note that there is also a parallel segmentation for this sentence (or part of it), as follows:

(12) Harry kissed Maxine and hugged Samantha

$$p_1 \qquad\qquad\qquad p_2$$

Harry must be excluded from p_1 since if it were to be included therein, condition (8b) would be violated: p_1 would be complete and p_2 incomplete. We will call an element not included in any p-segment, such as *Harry* in (11-12), a RESIDUE. Observe now that, while *Maxine* and *Samantha* may be analyzed as in relation only with the verbs of their respective p-segments (by the CSDC), *Harry* is allowed to act as an argument of both verbs without any violation of the CSDC or other principles of the theory. We will say that, in such a structure, the residue 'distributes across' both predicates. The principles of parallel segmentation thus provide for the correct analysis of this kind of structure as well.

Clearly parallel segmentation is the key to solving the domain problem for constructions of the type under discussion. But the nature of the solution is less simple than discussion thus far might cause it to appear. The reason can be seen from the following considerations: Obviously, to block spurious interpretations for sentences like (3) and (5), we must not only have the means to impose parallel segmentation upon them (with or without residue) but must guarantee that only the interpretations consistent with such a segmentation are to be permitted. That is, we must somehow indicate that not only is parallel segmentation of these sentences POSSIBLE, it is NECESSARY; merely defining parallel segmentation and providing an interpretation for it in terms of domain structure (via the CSDC) is insufficient in itself, since to do so does not logically entail that sentences like those under discussion have only the interpretations consistent with parallel segmentation. For these examples it would be sufficient merely to add the additional principle that if a sentence is subject to construal as an instance of parallel coordination, its range of interpretations is restricted to those consistent with its parallel segmentation. Unfortunately, such a requirement is too strong, as can be seen from consideration of a sentence like

(13)   Harry cooked and ate the fish.

This sentence is in two ways ambiguous, according as *cook* is construed as having a variable Object with null surface manifestation (as in *Harry cooked*) or as having *the fish* as its Object. The first interpretation is consistent with the following parallel segmentation:

(14)   Harry cooked and ate the fish

$$p_1 \qquad\qquad p_2$$

where p_1 is presumed to 'contain' an Object for *cook* by virtue of the possibility of interpreting the verb as having a null Object in this structure. (This possibility will, of course, not exist for all verbs.) Thus we obtain

the analysis

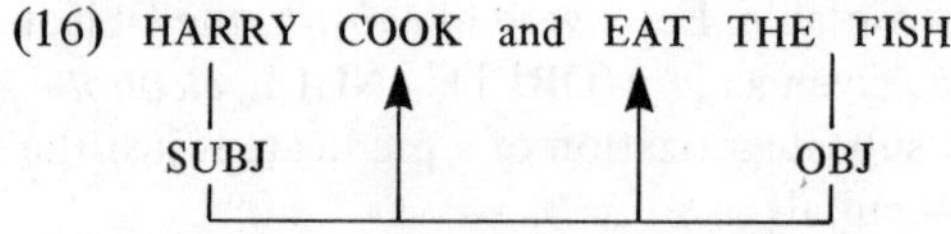

But the second analysis, i.e.,

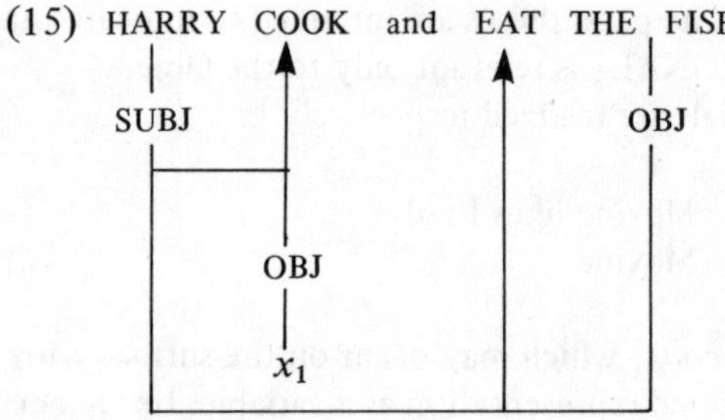

cannot arise from a parallel construal, since both NPs relate to both verbs; that is, under the analysis (16) the sentence must be construed as involving no partition into separate domains at all.

We are now on the horns of the following dilemma: Sentences (3,5) each have one interpretation consistent with parallel segmentation and hence must be construed exclusively as instances of parallel coordination; but sentence (13) illustrates a type of structure which may or may not be so construed. To restrict sentences susceptible to parallel segmentation to interpretation consistent with the segmentation will guarantee a unique interpretation for (3,5) but will incorrectly fail to allow the second interpretation of (13); on the other hand, simply to abandon the restriction will again open the door to spurious interpretations of (3,5).

An adequate compromise is available to remove the dilemma, but to render it intelligible, we must introduce a new notion — ARGUMENT POTENTIAL. Argument potential is related to strict subcategorization in the following way: Whereas the strict subcategorization of a predicate is an enumeration of the kinds of arguments it can take, each individual possibility in this enumeration is an argument potential. For example, the predicate *believe* must be subcategorized [+ *OBJ] and must also be marked as allowing both predicational and elementary Objects. We will represent the two potentials as [+ *(OBJ [+PREDICA-

TIONAL])] and [+*(OBJ[−PREDICATIONAL])], and the strict
subcategorization as [+ *(OBJ[+/−PREDICATIONAL])] (insofar
as Objects are involved). The parentheses are intended to indicate that
the feature [PREDICATIONAL] is relevant only to the Object
relation. The two potentials are realized respectively in

(17)　a.　Harry believes Maxine likes Fred.
　　　　b.　Harry believes Maxine.

Now consider a verb like *cook*, which may occur on the surface with a
null Object given in relational representation as a variable. Its Object
subcategorization may be given by the feature [+ *(OBJ[+/−NULL,
x_i])], where the inclusion of the symbol x_i is intended to indicate that
if the potential [+ *(OBJ[+NULL])] is realized, then OBJ*(cook)* = x_i,
i being the subscript of the variable. For a verb like *drink*, the Object
subcategorization would be given as [+ *(OBJ [+/−NULL, *alcoholic beverage*
Most succinctly, the strict subcategorization of a predicate is just the sum
of its distinct argument potentials.

The resolution of our dilemma lies in the following fact: There is a
built-in bias in grammar in favor of the realization of non-null argument
potentials. That is, in a structure containing a predicate having both null
and non-null potentials for a given relation, if the latter can be realized
under some analysis of the sentence, then the analysis in question must
be admitted. Thus, in a sentence like (13) the analysis (16), consistent
with a non-parallel construal, must be admitted, since it permits (though
it does not compel) realization of the non-null potential associated with
cook. On the other hand, it is not necessarily the case that analyses
allowing the realization of null argument potentials must always be
admitted. For example, the sentence

(18)　Harry cooked the rice and ate the fish.

could logically be analyzed as follows (consistent with a non-parallel
interpretation):

(19)　HARRY　COOK　THE RICE　and　EAT　THE　FISH

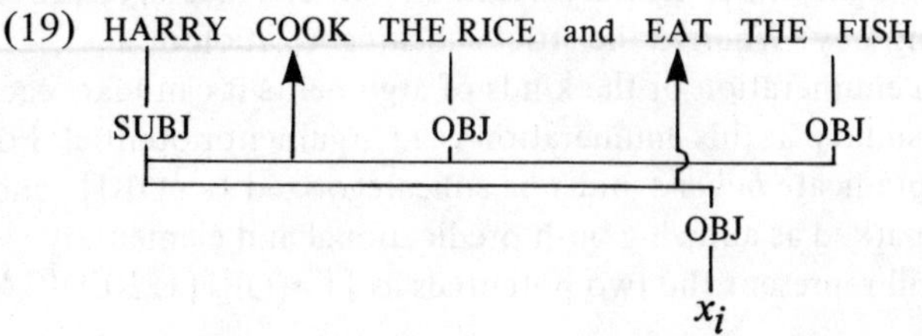

This analysis corresponds to an interpretation of (18) as a paraphrase of

(20) Harry cooked the fish and the rice, and ate.

But this interpretation is entirely spurious; even though it allows us to realize a particular potential for *eat* and does so in accordance with all principles of the theory so far introduced, it is not associable with (18).

We are now ready to state the principle which will correctly account for the facts presented thus far:

(21) PARALLEL SEGMENTATION IMPOSITION CONSTRAINT (PSIC)
    a. A sentence subject to construal as an instance of parallel coordination must have among its range of analyses all those consistent with the associated parallel segmentation.
    b. Such a sentence has additional analyses, not consistent with a parallel construal, if these analyses permit the realization of otherwise unrealizable NON-NULL argument potentials.

By PSIC-a, all sentences thus far considered will have readings consistent with parallel segmentation. By PSIC-b, (13) will have one further analysis, since this allows realization of a non-null Object potential for *cook* not realizable under parallel segmentation; but in the case of sentences such as (3, 5, 18) no non-null Object potential of the verbs involved goes unrealized under parallel segmentation, and these sentences are thus limited to the parallel construal.

The PSIC as formulated governs not only sentences such as (13) but also cases like

(22) Harry believes Fred and you talk too much.

which is ambiguous as between interpretations consistent with the analyses

(23) a. HARRY BELIEVE FRED and YOU TALK TOO MUCH

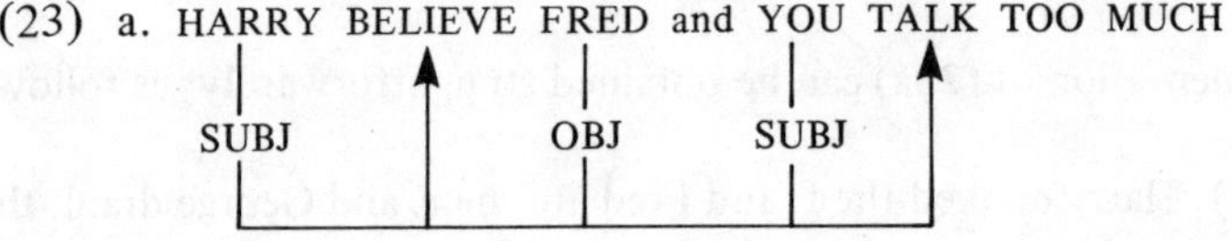

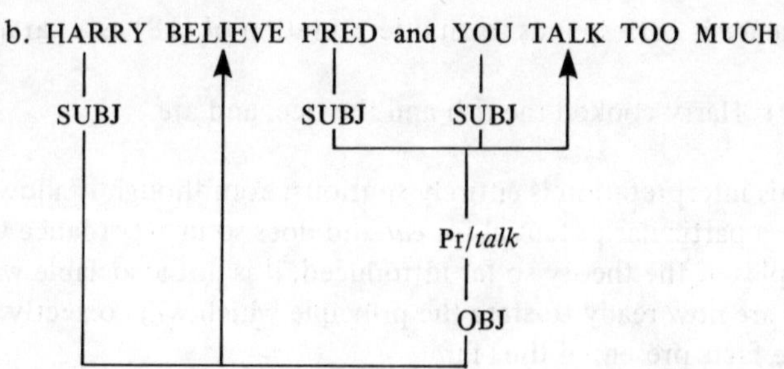

(This example was called to my attention by Larry Hutchinson.) The first analysis is consistent with the parallel segmentation

(24) Harry believes Fred and you talk too much
$$p_1 \qquad\qquad p_2$$

which permits realization of the Object potential [−NULL, −PRE-DICATIONAL] for *believe*; but *believe* also has the potential [−NULL, +PREDICATIONAL], and this can only be realized via a non-parallel construal. Thus, PSIC-b permits analysis (23b) to be obtained as well as (23a). (The ambiguity would, of course, be removed if a *that* were inserted after *believe,* since *talk* would then have to be analyzed as subordinate to some predicate.)

The foregoing establishes a means for assigning a domain structure to a certain class of coordinate structures. Thus far we have been concerned only with sentences containing two clauses; we must now consider polyclausal structures. We will examine two cases, as follows:

(25) a. Harry cooked the fish and Fred ate the rice and George drank the wine.

b. Harry cooked the fish and ate the rice and George drank the wine.

A segmentation of (25a) can be obtained straightforwardly, as follows:

(26) Harry cooked the f. and Fred ate the r. and George drank the w.
$$p_1 \qquad\qquad p_2 \qquad\qquad p_3$$

In the case of (25b), however, the situation is somewhat more complex.

A simple linear segmentation, i.e.,

(27) Harry cooked the f. and ate the r. and George drank the wine.

$$p_1 \qquad\qquad p_2 \qquad\qquad p_3$$

fails to satisfy condition (8b), since $p_{1,2}$ are incomplete while p_3 is complete. We need, therefore, a hierarchical arrangement:

(28) Harry cooked the f. and ate the r. and George drank the wine.

$$p_1 \qquad\qquad p_2$$

$$p_3 \qquad\qquad\qquad p_4$$

By grouping $p_{1,2}$ into a segment (which includes the distributing residue *Harry*), we create a complete segment which can then be conjoined to p_4; the hierarchical arrangement indicates that p_3 is subject to segmentation and that $p_{1,2}$ and the NP *Harry* are to be related only within p_3 and not with regard to the sentence as a whole. The admission of such hierarchical segmentations requires a slight modification of the CSDC, as follows:

(29) COORDINATE STRUCTURE DOMAIN CONSTRAINT –
Revised Formulation
No element contained within a p-segment may function as an argument of any predicate in another p-segment AT THE SAME HIERARCHICAL LEVEL.

Without the qualification, *Harry* could not distribute across *cook* and *eat*, since these predicates are contained in p-segments which do not contain *Harry*; nor could *the fish* and *the rice* be analyzed as Objects of their respective verbs, since they are contained in p_3 and hence, by the original formulation of the constraint, are not permitted to be in relation with predicates contained in other p-segments. But p_3 is at a different hierarchical level than $p_{1,2}$, and the modified constraint thus permits the correct analysis to be assigned.

All of the sentences discussed thus far have been susceptible to parallel construal. There are, however, sentences which do not involve parallelism at all, e.g., cases like

(30) a. Harry and Fred cooked the fish.
      b. Harry cooked the fish and the rice.
      c. Harry came and went.
      d. Harry and Fred came and went.

The analyses of (30a, b, c) are straightforward — indeed, they could be accomplished entirely via C-rules and metaconditions. A sentence like (30d), however, is problematical. The correct analysis is

(31) HARRY and FRED COME and GO

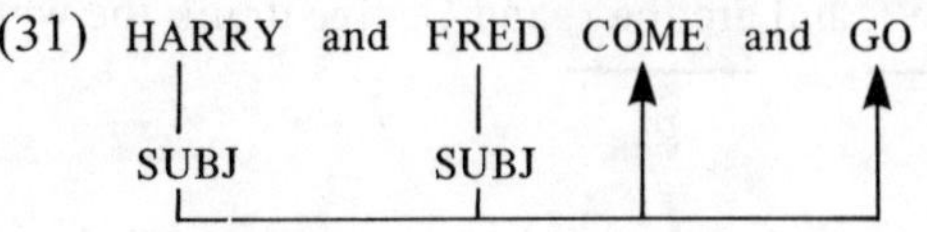

In other words, both NPs distribute across the two predicates; but the apparatus available thus far would also permit two non-distributive analyses, i.e.,

(32) a. HARRY and FRED COME and GO

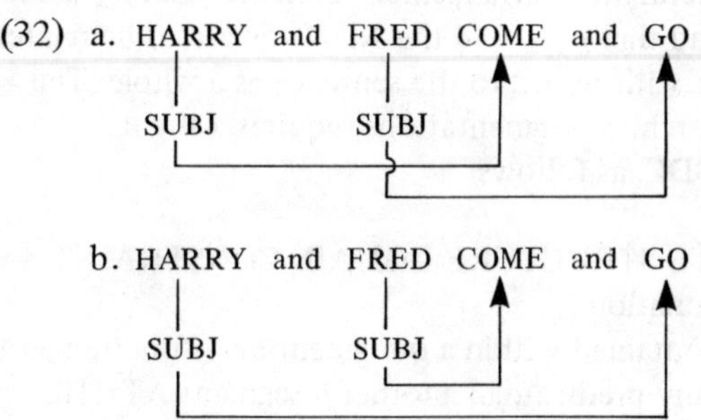

      b. HARRY and FRED COME and GO

To rule out these incorrect interpretations, we must adopt a constraint which I will call the Law of Distribution:

(33) LAW OF DISTRIBUTION
      Any element in a coordinate structure which is (a) not included in any *p*-segment and (b) is analyzed as $a(P)$, where P is one of a series of coordinate predicates, must be analyzed as in relation a to ALL predicates in the coordinate series insofar as subcategorization permits — EXCEPT when *respectively* follows the coordinate series.[2]

This will force both NPs in (30d) to distribute across both predicates in the sentence. The qualification 'in so far as subcategorization permits' is pertinent to cases like

(34) Harry came and visited Maxine.

where *Maxine* must be analyzed as OBJ*(visit)* but does not distribute, since *come* is intransitive.

Additional motivation for the Law of Distribution derives from sentences like the following:

(35) *Harry, Fred likes Maxine and hates Samantha.

This sentence is susceptible to the following parallel segmentation:

(36) *Harry, Fred likes Maxine and hates Samantha

$$p_1 \qquad\qquad p_2$$

Without the Law of Distribution, *Harry* could act as Subject of one predicate and *Fred* as Subject of the other; but the Law of Distribution requires that each NP be in relation to each predicate, which leads to a Uniqueness violation. Thus, (35) is predicted to be ill-formed by virtue of overloading, which is precisely the desired result. (Addition of *respectively* to the sentence will not change its status, since *Harry* and *Fred* are not coordinate, as they would have to be in a well-formed *respectively*-coordination.)

The introduction of the Law of Distribution raises a further problem, however, namely, that of defining precisely the conditions under which two predicates are coordinate. The reason can be seen if we consider a sentence such as

(37) Harry believes George and Max like Fred.

which is unambiguous, having only the analysis

(38)

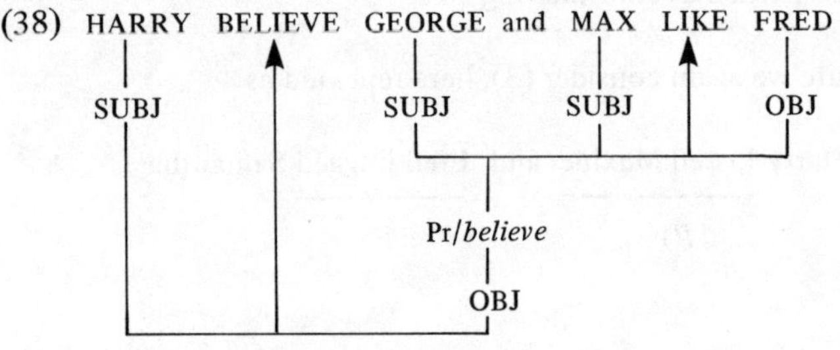

In dealing with such a sentence, we face the following difficulty: Observe first that, since *and* intervenes between *believe* and *like*, it is possible in principle to construe these predicates as loosely coordinate; and if they are so construed, then the Law of Distribution will require (among other things) that *Harry* be analyzed as Subject of both verbs, as must *George* and *Max*. That this possibility would be ruled out by other constraints (note, for example, that *Harry* and *George* are not coordinate, so there will be a Uniqueness violation) does not resolve the problem, since if the Law of Distribution applies to such sentences as this, then (37) is erroneously predicted to be ill-formed by virtue of violating said constraints. Since the sentence is in fact well-formed, there being no distribution of NPs across the two predicates, we are forced to the conclusion that the predicates are not coordinate. On the other hand, the predicates in (35) must be construed as coordinate, if our account of the basis for the ill-formedness of the sentence is correct.

There are no doubt many possible ways to resolve this difficulty. The one to be adopted here is taken because, as will be seen later, it contributes to the solution of another problem. It involves adopting the following condition on the interpretation of conjunctions that occur between predicates:

(39)   A coordinating conjunction coordinates predicates iff the predicates in question are thereby strictly coordinated or enter into *p*-segments that are thereby strictly coordinated.

Observe that neither condition is met in the case of (37); hence, the *and* cannot be construed as coordinating the two predicates, and the Law of Distribution is inapplicable. One of the conditions is, however, met by each of the other relevant examples.

The opposite side of the coin is represented by the following conditions:

(40)   A conjunction which coordinates predicates cannot be construed as coordinating NPs.

To illustrate we again consider (3), here repeated as

(41)   Harry kissed Maxine and Fred hugged Samantha
$$\underline{\hspace{4cm}}\qquad\underline{\hspace{4cm}}$$
$$p_1\qquad\qquad\qquad p_2$$

The segmentation is logically possible and yet incorrect; if it were admissible, we could obtain the spurious analysis

(42) HARRY KISS MAXINE and FRED HUG SAMANTHA

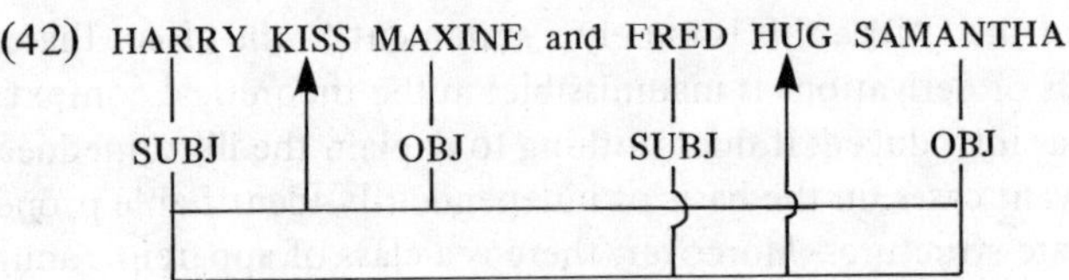

According to this analysis, (41) could be construed as having as one of its readings the interpretation of

(43) Harry kissed Maxine and Samantha, and Harry and Fred
      hugged Samantha.

Such an interpretation would be possible without the constraint (41) by virtue of the fact that both *Harry* and *Samantha* would be required to distribute, Uniqueness violations being prevented by the possibility of taking the pairs *Harry, Fred* and *Maxine, Samantha* as loosely coordinate.

For convenience we will combine (39-40) under the general heading of the COORDINATE PREDICATE CONSTRAINT:

(44) COORDINATE PREDICATE CONSTRAINT (CPC)
      a. A coordinating conjunction coordinates predicates iff the
         predicates in question are thereby strictly coordinated
         or enter into *p*-segments that are thereby strictly
         coordinated.
      b. A coordinating conjunction that coordinates predicates may
         not be construed as coordinating NPs.

5.2. The Coordinate Structure Constraint: an Explanation of the Facts

In the foregoing section we developed a series of principles to solve the domain problem for coordinate structures. Though this apparatus is probably incomplete, it is sufficient to provide us with a basis for explaining, rather than merely providing a representational account of, the body of facts motivating the inclusion of Ross's Coordinate Structure Constraint (CSC) in TG. As stated by Ross (1967), the CSC is as follows:

(45) COORDINATE STRUCTURE CONSTRAINT
      In a coordinate structure no conjunct may be moved, nor

may any element contained in a conjunct be moved out of that conjunct.

As is true of the CNPC, this is merely a statement to the effect that a certain class of derivations is inadmissible; in the theoretical context in which it was introduced, it does nothing to explain the ill-formedness of the relevant cases on the basis of independently identifiable properties of coordinate structures. Moreover, there is a class of apparent counter-examples to the constraint, e.g.,

(46) a. Maxine, Harry came and saw.
      b. The lute, Harry sings madrigals and plays.

Both sentences are well-formed and would normally be analyzed transformationally as arising from movement of the initial NP from the second conjunct. Ross attempts to escape this difficulty by regarding such structures as non-coordinate at a certain level of analysis, though the problems of such a strategy are clear and have been noted elsewhere (Rodman 1971, Grosu 1972).

It will be shown below that the facts noted by Ross, including the "exceptions", are automatic consequences of general principles governing coordinate structures, principally directed toward the solution of the domain problem for well-formed coordinations. All but one of these principles have already been introduced in the preceding section; the one that has not yet been introduced is relevant to cases like

(47) a. Harry likes Fred and Maxine.
      b. ≠ *Maxine, Harry likes Fred and.

The principle is an obvious one: coordinating conjunctions must conjoin, and, in English at least, this requires that they occur between conjuncts.[3] Thus a case of this sort is perhaps the easiest to deal with. A more interesting instance is provided by sentence pairs such as

(48) a. Harry came and Fred went.
      b. ≠ *Fred, Harry came and went.

Here, the Law of Distribution is crucially involved; indeed, (48b) is simply the intransitive analogue of (35). By CPC-a, *come* and *go* are coordinate, and by the Law of Distribution both NPs must act as Subjects of both verbs; but these NPs are not coordinate or coreferential, and thus the Law of Uniqueness is violated by such an analysis. (Addition of *respectively* fails to render the sentence well-formed for the same reason it fails to do so in the case of (35).) The relationship between (35) and (48b) is important for the following reason: It seems plausible to regard the two sentences, which are very similar in form, as ill-formed for the same reason; they are indeed so treated by our principles, which force them both to be viewed as instances of over-loading. But in a standard transformational account, only (48b) could be regarded as ill-formed on grounds of movement; (35) would be ill-formed by virtue of overloading, whether or not it were viewed as derived via movement. Thus, we are able to capture a significant generalization in a corepresentational treatment of the facts which goes entirely unrecognized by a standard transformational one.

Consider now one of the 'exceptional' cases, i.e., (46a), repeated here as

(49) Maxine, Harry came and saw. (=Harry came and saw Maxine.)

The reason that this sentence is well-formed, even though its derivation violates the CSC, lies in the fact that, whereas in (48) we are dealing with coordinate intransitive verbs, here one verb is transitive and the other intransitive. The analysis of (49) is

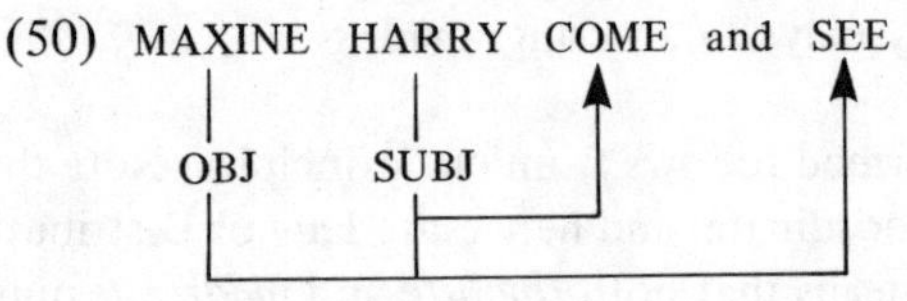

(50) MAXINE HARRY COME and SEE

OBJ   SUBJ

which violates no relevant principles. Since *come* is not transitive, *Maxine* does not distribute; but, since both predicates require Subjects, *Harry* does distribute. The resulting analysis does not lead to any Uniqueness violation, and hence there is no overloading in such a structure.

Consider now (46b) repeated as

(51) The lute, Harry sings madrigals and plays.
        (= Harry sings madrigals and plays the lute.)

Here, the correct analysis is

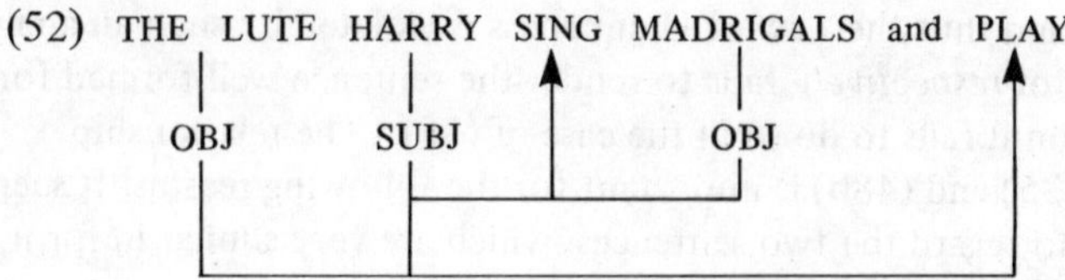

Note that the sentence is not subject to any parallel segmentation and also that its predicates are not strictly coordinate. Hence, by the CPC the predicates are not coordinate at all, and the Law of Distribution in inapplicable. This explains why *madrigals* can be analyzed as Object of *sing* only, and *the lute* as Object of *play* only, even though both verbs are transitive.[4] Since the analysis (52) satisfies all relevant principles, (51) is well-formed under the assigned interpretation.

Now consider the paradigm

(53) a. Harry plays the lute and sings madrigals.
b. (*) The lute, Harry plays and sings madrigals.

The asterisk on (53b) is in parentheses, since there are two renderings of this sentence depending on placement of the major intonation break. They are

(54) a. *The lute / / Harry plays and sings madrigals.
b. The lute, Harry plays / / and sings madrigals.

That (54a) should be ill-formed follows from our principles. Note that *play* and *sing* are strictly coordinate, and hence the Law of Distribution is applicable; this in turn means that both *the lute* and *madrigals* must be construed as Objects of both verbs. But by virtue of coordinating predicates, the *and* cannot coordinate these two NPs, and hence the Law of Uniqueness is violated.

The sentence may be re-rendered as (54b) however, with an attendant increase in acceptability. This fact remains to be explained. To see what is involved, we consider two renderings of a sentence of partially similar form:

(55) a. Harry plays and sings madrigals.
b. Harry plays / / and sings madrigals.

Note that in (55b) the intonation break before *and* has a strong inhibitory effect on the distribution of *madrigals* as Object across both verbs — though it has no such effect on the |distribution of *Harry* as Subject. It seems plausible to suppose that a similar sort of inhibitory effect obtains in (54b), where the intonation break is in an analogous position. Thus, despite strict coordination of predicates, the two Object NPs need not distribute, and no Uniqueness violation need ensue. Accordingly, the Law of Distribution requires the addition of one further mitigating clause; I will not attempt a precise statement here, since the general question of the precise role of intonation in coordinate structures requires further and more detailed investigation.

If the foregoing discussion is correct, then we have another important item of support for the corepresentational position. In particular, we have another class of facts which suggest that the notions 'predicate domain' and 'domain restriction', as applied to surface structure, have a significant place in grammatical theory. In so far as such notions have a role in TG, they are considered to be relevant only to an abstract, normalized underlying structure (at least traditionally — but see Cattell 1976). It has been the goal of this chapter and the two preceding ones to argue that relational (and hence predicational) structure not only CAN but SHOULD be defined directly on surface syntactic objects rather than on hypothetical abstract ones. I have no doubts that the approach developed here will be much improved by subsequent research and that the foregoing is best viewed as a beginning attack on the domain problem in natural language; none the less, it seems to me that the fact that interesting results follow even from so crude an apparatus as that constructed in these chapters augurs well for subsequent research from a corepresentational point of view and the refinements that it will inevitably bring.

5.3. Some Remarks on Gapping

The phenomenon of gapping has special relevance to this discussion, since it has recently been argued (Hankamer 1973) that gapped sentences provide particularly strong evidence for transformations. More precisely, Hankamer presents arguments to the effect that gapped constructions must be derived from full coordinations by a deletion transformation; it is therefore of interest to consider a corepresentational treatment of such constructions in the light of these arguments.

Let us first consider how a treatment of gapped sentences might be implemented in a CORG framework. Such a treatment is possible given the following rule:

(56) ANALOGOUS ORDER RULE
The relative order of marked and unmarked arguments in the elliptical conjunct of a gapped construction must match that in the full conjunct.

Such a rule will account for the semantic anomaly of a sentence like

(57) *Harry drank wine, and vodka Fred.

since, according to the rule, the only analysis can be

(58) HARRY DRINK WINE and VODKA FRED

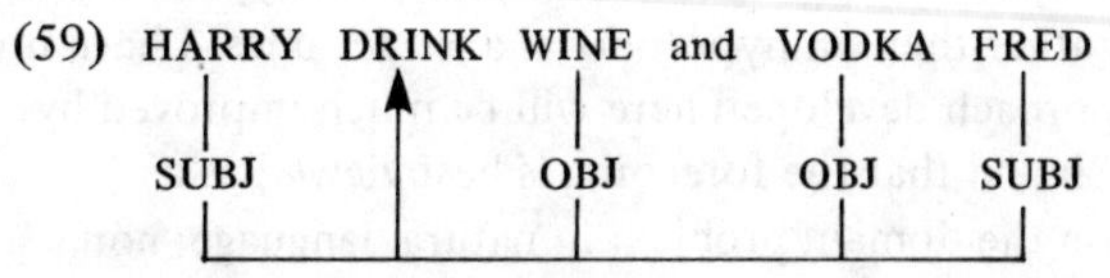

and selectional restrictions on *drink* are thereby violated. Without this rule, it would be possible to impose the analysis

(59) HARRY DRINK WINE and VODKA FRED

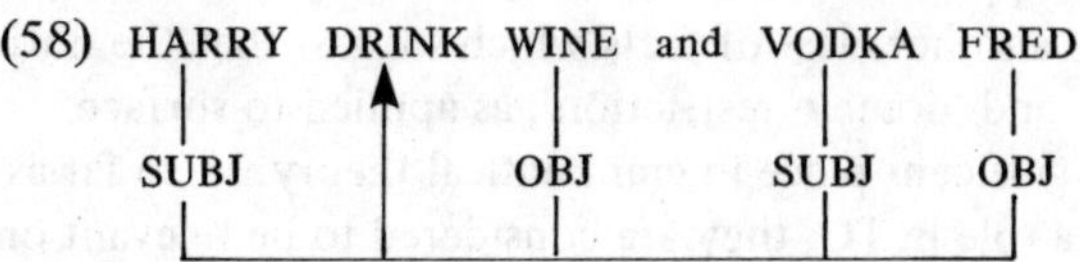

according to which, there ought to be a reading on which the sentence is well-formed.

The Analogous Order Rule also prohibits such sentences as

(60) *Wine was drunk by Harry, and vodka Fred.

Since *drink* occurs here in passive form, its Subject is marked; thus, in order to satisfy the rule, we must take *vodka* as unmarked and *Fred* as marked. But this violates the Passive Subject Rule, which requires that an overtly occurring passive Subject be the Object of *by*, and *Fred* does not meet this requirement. Now compare

(61) a. *Wine was drunk by Harry, and by Fred vodka.
b. By Harry, wine was drunk, and by Fred, vodka.

Sentence (61a) is ill-formed because *Fred,* even though OBJ(*by*), is in the wrong position: the order in the second conjunct must be

u-ARG–m-ARG. In (61b), however, the order m-ARG–u-ARG obtains in the first conjunct and thus may also obtain in the second.[5]

The Analogous Order Rule corresponds to the condition on a transformationally formulated gapping rule requiring identity between predicates of the underlying full-conjuncts — which condition blocks the application of the transformation when one predicate is active and one is passive. One type of case that has yet to be considered is

(62) *Harry likes Maxine, and Fred by Samantha.

In a transformational treatment such a sentence would be underivable via Gapping, since it would require deletion of a passive predicate in the second conjunct while the corresponding predicate in the full conjunct is active. In a corepresentational treatment such a sentence would be ruled out by virtue of the fact that no argument of *like* in active may be marked by a preposition.

We thus see that the correct generalizations about the relational structure of gapped constructions can be made in a CORG-based treatment of English without any difficulty. We are now ready to consider Hankamer's arguments in favor of a transformational treatment:

Argument 1

In German, there are certain idiosyncratic exceptions to the usual rule of case marking, as illustrated by

(63) a. Das Kind folgte *mir*, und der Hund *meinem* Vater.
          'The child followed *me* (Dative), and the dog *my* (Dative) father.'

      b. *Das Kind folgte *mir*, und der Mund *meinen* Vater.

                    (Dat.)   (Ace.)

The point here is that with the verb in question the Object normally takes the Dative rather than the expected Accusative case. Hankamer's reasoning proceeds as follows: Since a special case marking rule must be given for such verbs in any event so as to account for full sentences like

(64) Der Hund folgte meinem Vater.

the correct case assignment will follow automatically if (a) gapped conjuncts are derived from corresponding full cases and (b) Gapping is ordered after Case Marking.[6]

Argument 2

A comparable argument can be constructed on the basis of preposition selection with certain verbs. As a relevant example, consider

(65) Das Kind fürchtet *vor* dem Hund, und die Frau *vor* der Maus.
'The child fears *(for)* the dog, and the woman *(for)* the mouse.'

where no preposition other than *vor* is permitted. An analogous English example is

(66) Bill depends *on* Alex and Alex *on* Bill.

In either case, there must be a rule requiring the marking of the Object of the verb with specific preposition; such rules are much like the case government conditions just considered, and hence the same sorts of conclusions may be drawn.

Argument 3

A third argument, similar to the other two, involves selectional restrictions. In a sentence like

(67) *Jack admires chastity, and sincerity the bedpost.

the ill-formedness of the sentence as a whole may be accounted for naturally if the second conjunct derives from

(68) *Sincerity admires the bedpost.

In all three cases of this sort, Hankamer claims, 'direct' generation of the gapped sentences would lead to an account lacking in explanatory power. Special devices must be added in order to handle case government, preposition selection, and verb-argument co-occurrence in gapped conjuncts, whereas no such additional devices will be needed in a transformationally based account. Moreover, he maintains, the transformational account predicts that the facts should be exactly as they are — that is, that the restrictions applying to gapped sentences should be parallel to those applying to the corresponding full cases; given direct generation of the elliptical sentences, the possibility would be allowed for in principle that gapped and full conjuncts might differ in this respect.

Argument 4

Here we quote directly:

> The basic fact to be accounted for is that every elliptical sentence is a truncated version of some well-formed nonelliptical sentence. That is to say, every elliptical sentence consists of constituents which can occur as parts of some ordinary sentence, in the order in which they would occur in the ordinary sentence. If [the elliptical clauses of gapped sentences are generated directly], this generalization is lost. [p. 20]

Let us examine these four arguments in order. To counter the first, it suffices merely to show that there is a way of capturing the generaliz-ations in question without recourse to a deletion rule. That this is possible in CORG can easily be shown. Observe first that it is possible to write rules for Object case marking according to the following schema:

(69)   If NP_i = $OBJ(P_j)$, mark NP_i with case K

For languages like German, the 'normal' Object case will be Accusative; for certain predicates, however, K will have to be Dative. For each class of verbs relative to case assignment, there will have to be a rule in the form (69). Let us now return to Hankamer's examples, comparing

(70)   a. Das Kind folgte mir und der Hund meinem/*meinen Vater.
       b. Das Kind folgte mir und der Hund folgte meinem/*meinen Vater.

In both cases, given our principles for analyzing gapped sentences, *meinem(*n) Vater* will be marked OBJ*(folgte)*; it is of absolutely no consequence whether or not a second occurrence of the verb appears in the sentence. But given that the relevant case assignment rule is an instantiation of the schema (69), one rule will suffice for both full and gapped sentences. Moreover, the prediction that elliptical and full sentences will behave exactly the same way in regard to|case govern-ment is still maintained — since the relevant NP must be analyzed as maintaining the relation OBJ to the predicate in either instance. Exactly analogous replies may be made to arguments 2 and 3.

Argument 4 may be countered by pointing out that it makes an assumption that happens to be factually incorrect. It is not true that elliptical sentences always have well-formed full counterparts. There are, for example, languages with truncated passives but not full passive constructions. The imperative construction in French provides a second counterexample. The sentence

(71) Allez y.
       'Go ahead.'

can be rendered only in the form in which it is given in (71); it is not possible to add an overt second person Subject pronoun, as in

(72) *Vous allez y.

Nor is it the case that the order of constituents in elliptical sentences need be the same as in full sentences. Once again, French illustrates: There are a number of verbs in French which involve an empty reflexive — e.g. *s'assoir* 'to sit' (literally 'to seat oneself'). In declaratives, this reflexive (which is normally clitic) must precede the verb:

(73) Vous vous asseyez.
       'You sit' (Declarative)

In imperatives, however, the clitic reflexive must follow the verb (there being a general constraint in French prohibiting clitics from occurring sentence-initially):

(74) Asseyez vous.
       'Sit down/be seated'

Both of the following are ungrammatical:

(75) a. *Vous asseyez vous.
       b. *Vous vous asseyez. (as imperative)

No doubt similar examples can be found in other languages, and on this basis I question the force of Hankamer's fourth argument.

It would appear in general that the facts pertaining to gapping fail to support a transformational approach uniquely. (In this connection it might be noted that another recent attempt at defending the claim that transformational deletion rules are necessary — Grinder and Postal 1971 — can also be shown to fail. See Kac 1972c for a demonstration of this fact.) In general, I would question the extent to which the general argument form employed by Hankamer, which exploits real or imagined analogies between elliptical and full constructions, provides a viable means of supporting the transformationalist position.

Notes

1. Since the completion of this study, further investigation of coordinate structure from a corepresentational point of view has been carried out by Justin Holl, who suggests that the apparatus developed here can be reduced to more elementary principles. In view of the preliminary nature of the results so far, I have not incorporated them into this chapter, though the line of attack seems promising and may well be successful in the near future.
2. The rule for *respectively* coordination is, roughly speaking, that the *i*th in a series of coordinate NPs stands in relation with the *i*th in the series of coordinate predicates; thus, if *respectively* were appended to (30d), (32a) would be the correct analysis.
3. A problem none the less exists, as Justin Holl has reminded me, with sentences like *And now — here's Johnny!* Although one tends to enter treacherous ground with such proposals, I feel that cases like this may be treated via something like a presuppositional analysis, taking into account features of pragmatic context. Such a sentence can be analyzed as conveying the message 'You've been waiting impatiently for Johnny, and now, here he is', the first clause representing a statement of the presupposition which renders the use of initial *and* appropriate. Just how such an analysis is to be formalized remains to be seen.
4. There are two spurious analyses which must be ruled out for such a sentence, i.e.:

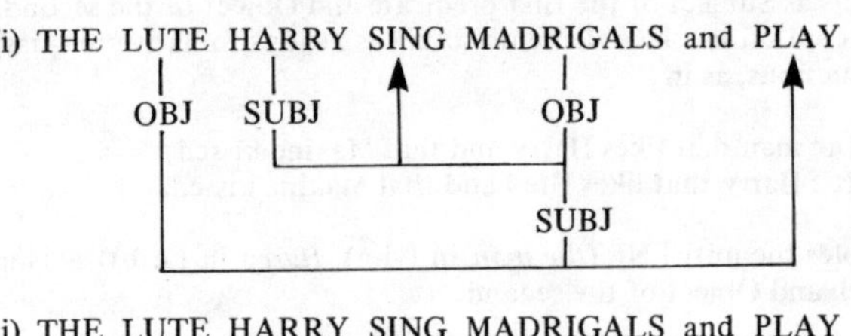

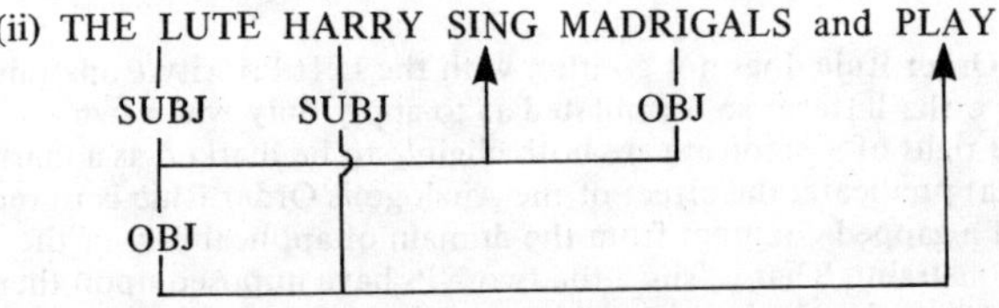

Ignoring the matter of selectional restrictions (examples can be readily constructed of the same form in which comparable analyses do not lead to selectional violations), we may bring the following considerations to bear:

In the case of (i), we have a violation of an independently motivated constraint which prohibits configurations of the form

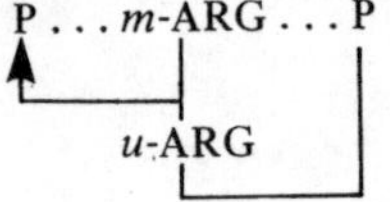

So, for example, in

(iii)   Harry saw a bear and ran.

SUBJ*(run)* can only be *Harry*, not *a bear*.
   With regard to (ii), the relevant constraint is one which, except in two
situations to be described below, prohibits configurations of the form

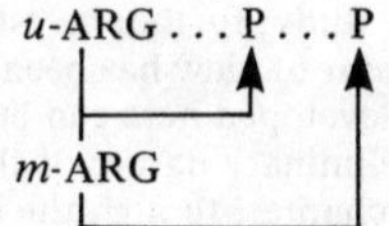

The following examples illustrate; in each, *Harry* acts as Subject of the first
predicate and ought, in principle, to be analyzable via the ODC as Object
of the second:

(iv)   a. *Harry believes that Maxine likes.
        b. *Harry knows a girl who likes.
        c. *Harry arrived and Maxine kissed.

In all three cases, the analysis in question is blocked, and an incomplete
domain for the second verb results, since no Object can be located.
   The first of the two exceptional situations is represented by T-predicates
(see §2.5), as in

(v)   Harry is tough to please.

Here, *Harry* acts as Subject of the first predicate and Object of the second.
The second exception involves elements acting as heads of relative or quasi-
relative constructions, as in

(vi)   a. the man that likes Harry and that Maxine kissed
        b. It's Harry that likes Fred and that Maxine kissed.

In both examples the initial NP (*the man* in (vi a), *Harry* in (vi b)) acts as Subject
of the first verb and Object of the second.

5. The Analogous Order Rule does not conflict with the Left Priority Constraint
   (§3.2.3.1), since the latter is so formulated as to apply only when two
   elements to the right of a predicate are both eligible to be marked as a marked
   argument of that predicate; the effect of the Analogous Order Rule is to remove
   the elements of a gapped conjunct from the domain of applicability of the
   Left Priority Constraint. That is, since the two NPs have imposed upon them
   the requirement that they be interpreted in a particular way with regard to
   argument markedness, the possibility of any other interpretation is precluded.
6. This ordering will be automatic if the principle of Obligatory-Optional
   Precedence (Ringen 1972) is included in transformational theory.

6 METATHEORETICAL FOUNDATIONS

6.1. Retrospect

In the preceding four chapters, we implemented a method for mapping between categorial and relational representations in simplex and complex sentences. The notions 'predication manifestation', 'predicate domain', and 'domain restriction' played a fundamental role in the development of the method and were claimed to be terms of a metalanguage better suited to the matters at hand than that provided by transformational theory. In particular, it was argued that the strategy of defining predicate domains on surface structures makes possible an explanatory account of a number of phenomena, where such an explanation is unavailable in standard transformational accounts. This in turn suggests that properties of surface structure must receive considerably more emphasis than TG has traditionally accorded them.

Like TG, CORG is deeply rooted in traditional ways of thinking about language. The type of analysis for which it provides a set of formal principles is anything but novel, having been carried out in countless schoolroom exercises over many hundreds of years. It goes without saying, of course, that there is no inherent scientific interest in formalizing this kind of analysis merely to lend it an aura of legitimacy or to 'show it can be done'; nor should the claims made here be taken as in any way justifying the endless progression of dreary chores imposed on the young by the Miss Fidditches of the world. Any system of grammatical analysis is of interest only to the extent that it contributes to some understanding of linguistic phenomena.

For the remainder of this chapter, I will consider the claims advanced in this study in a broader context. Beginning with an attempt to meet two anticipated objections, I then will move to a comparison of what may be called 'formalist' with 'notionalist', or 'conceptualist', theories of grammar and will argue that the latter, which has been somewhat eclipsed in the recent history of linguistics, deserves to be revived.

6.2. Two Anticipated Objections

6.2.1. Psychological Implications

One possible objection to the foregoing might run as follows:
Even granting the validity of all the claims made above, TG is none the

less secure, since CORG is concerned with performance rather than competence — i.e., with mechanisms of sentence processing rather than with the internalized knowledge of the speaker-hearer. Since TG is centrally concerned with competence, it cannot be undermined by any of the findings reported here. Moreover, since CORG is concerned only with processing, it is incomplete even as a performance model, since such a model must also have a production component.

There are numerous ways of replying to such a hypothetical objection. I will take the opportunity here to use this issue as background for arguing against a widespread misconception as to the relationship between linguistic and psychological theories.

I begin by denying that CORG is a theory of performance, but I also deny that it is a theory of competence; it is, rather, a theory of linguistic STRUCTURE, i.e., of the organizational principles of linguistic systems which must be understood before it even makes sense to speak of how languages are known, learned, or used. Furthermore, I could claim that TG has exactly the same status; like CORG, it must be taken as a theory of structure rather than of competence.[1] To show that even a correct description of linguistic structure (i.e., a description which generates the language and is in accord with native speaker intuitions about the language) cannot be automatically assumed to be a description of any speaker's actual knowledge, I here briefly summarize a parable due to Hutchinson (1974) which makes the point quite neatly. Suppose we are confronted by a computer which is producing a certain type of output — say statements of the form $x + y = z$. The 'competence' of the computer may be identified with its program — a system of instructions which, if properly carried out, will enable the machine to produce all and only well-formed statements of the form in question (by 'well-formed' I here mean 'admissible by the formation rules of elementary arithmetic and true'). The 'performance' of the machine consists of all actual productions, including the production of occasional garbage which may result from defects or breakdowns of hardware. The question that must be asked is this: Suppose we were to write a program for ordinary addition; this program, if it worked, would in some sense account for the output of the computer, since it, like the computer's program, would generate all and only well-formed statements in the form $x + y = z$. Would we have thereby characterized the competence of the machine? This question reduces to the question 'Having written program P for ordinary addition and knowing that P will generate exactly the same non-garbage output as that produced by the computer, are we thereby entitled to assume that P is the program employed by the computer?' The answer, clearly, is 'No'. There are infinitely many algorithms for the manipulation of any formal system and hence infinitely many possible ways of programming a machine to operate with the system. Thus, to show sufficiency of P to generate the correct output is to show nothing relative to the actual program of the computer in the parable. Moreover, recourse to such notions as 'simplicity', 'explanatory adequacy', and so on will not necessarily justify one hypothesis over another as to the nature of the machine's program, since what is ideal from a mathematical or aesthetic point of view may be far from ideal for the machine itself. For example, very complicated, unaesthetic, and unrevealing algorithms may be highly desirable from a machine standpoint if they have 'performance' value of a certain kind − e.g., if they minimize computation time. By the same token, a very simple and intuitively satisfying algorithm from a mathematical point of view may be grossly inefficient as the basis for a practical program. The moral is that formal analysis of output is itself insufficient to determine the precise nature of the competence of the device producing the output.[2] But most linguistic investigation within a generative framework has proceeded in essentially this way; the writer of a transformational grammar, or a portion of such a grammar, having demonstrated its sufficiency to account for a set of facts, then infers that this grammar must represent the knowledge of speakers of the language for which it is written. But to show sufficiency for such a grammar, even if it is highly revealing, is not to show that any human speaker's competence is actually an instance of this grammar.[3]

This does not, however, mean that the task of writing generative grammars is a pointless or futile one − even as currently carried out. We must merely adjust our conception of what grammars are really intended to account for. If we regard grammars as accounts of structure rather than of speaker competence, the conventional *modus operandi* of generative linguistic investigation is entirely appropriate. The question of how a language is organized (which is the same as the question of what its structure is) is a different one from that of how a speaker comes to be able to use it − though in answering the first we contribute to some extent to the answer to the second, since it is precisely the fact that languages have structure that renders them knowable and learnable in the first place. I argue elsewhere (Kac 1974b) that a valid conception of linguistic structure is prerequisite to, and therefore independent of, any psychological account of human linguistic capacity. The rationale, in encapsulated form, is simply that it makes no sense in my view to ask questions pertaining to learning and knowledge without a reliable prior understanding of the essential nature of the things learned or known. But this prior understanding must then be independent of any theory of learning or knowledge, since otherwise the entire enterprise is prejudiced and circular. The linguistic case is peculiar in one respect, of course, namely, that language is itself a mental product and thus has no existence independent of human beings — unlike, say, physical phenomena. But this fact (which I have no wish to deny) cannot be taken as justifying a vicious circle; though the assumption that languages can be studied as if they did have user-independent status embodies a fiction, it is a fiction of convenience to which I see no alternative if the study of human psychology is to have any content.

To return now to the original objection, I view CORG and TG as alternative metalanguages for the characterization of linguistic structure, to be compared as to the extent to which they lead to hypotheses revealing of the nature of linguistic structure. The notions 'competence' and 'performance' are irrelevant to this comparison. Both metalanguages provide frameworks within which to make statements of the form 'Natural languages are systems having property p', the correctness or incorrectness of such statements being determinable on the basis of the normal criteria for the evaluation of theories: consistency with known facts and ability to predict further ones, freedom from internal contradiction, generality, explanatory power, and so on. To say that one metalanguage is preferable to another is simply to say that one biases linguistic investigation in a more viable way than the other, i.e., that one leads more directly to the discovery of viable hypotheses by virtue of the specific manner in which it defines problems and suggests criteria for possible solutions to these problems. Having given a satisfactory account of linguistic structure, we then proceed to consideration of the manner in which human beings come to master their languages. A prior and independently justified conception of structure is a powerful tool in this type of investigation, since it provides a touchstone against which specific psychological accounts can be tested: the range of valid psychological hypotheses can be limited to just those which are consistent with what is actually known about the structure of language. While other criteria must then be brought to bear in selecting the correct alternative, it is at least possible to rule out in advance a large number of incorrect hypotheses by virtue of their lack of fit with a structural model that has been independently validated.

As a postscript to the foregoing, I would like to comment briefly on the relationship between CORG and the theory of 'perceptual strategies' currently being explored by some investigators. On one level, there is little to distinguish the two, since both may be regarded as attempting to answer the following question: To what structural information must a language user have access in order to understand the sentences of his or her language? In so far as we are claiming that a variety of facts of interpretation may be explained via recourse to such notions as 'argument segment', 'status', 'parallel segmentation', etc., and to specific principles that refer to these notions (such as the Similarity Constraint or the Law of Distribution), then we are claiming that actual language processing is explicated in part in these terms. At another level, however, there is an important difference. I take the term 'perceptual strategy' to refer literally to a procedure actually used by a speaker to decode a sentence with regard to a particular type of information encoded therein. Since CORG is not intended as a theory of performance, it cannot be regarded as specifying such procedures; therefore, the steps that are gone through to establish the analysis of a sentence are not to be taken as analogues to those gone through by speakers performing the same task. Rather, CORG seeks only to specify the contribution made by surface syntactic structure to the outcome of the decoding operation. The nature of the operation itself is properly the province of the psychologist, not the linguist.

It is worth pointing out that in actual fact most so-called 'perceptual strategies' do not conform to the literal sense of the term. They are less statements of processing operations than statements of correlations between surface configurations and interpretations – much like the C-rules of a corepresentational grammar. I thus question the felicitousness of the term 'perceptual strategy', since a surface-inter-. pretation correlation is not identifiable with an operation. This is not to deny, of course, that a theory of such correlations (which CORG attempts to provide) is a necessary first step in arriving at an under-standing of these operations.

6.2.2. The System of Relations

In this section I take up the question of the justification for the Subject/ Object dichotomy in representing the relational structure of predications. Since the advent of case grammar (Fillmore 1968, 1969), many investig-ators have taken the view that the relations Subject and Object have only 'surface' significance and that 'deep' grammatical structure requires access to a more variegated array of predicate-argument relations than the traditional 'grammatical relations' provide. (For a recent set of arguments to the effect that the notions Logical Subject/Object are not required in grammatical theory, see Norman 1974.) It might well be asked, then, why CORG continues to maintain the relations (Logical) Subject/Object.

In answering this question, I want to emphasize that I see no point in attempting to argue AGAINST the validity of the assumption that at some level of analysis a system of relations involving notions like Fillmore's cases will be necessary. Nor can I at present claim that there is extensive substantive motivation FOR making reference to the relations Subject and Object as defined here. For the moment, let me simply point out that such notions as 'Agent', 'Patient', 'Experiencer', 'Goal', and so on are commonly misconstrued; whereas these relations are commonly thought of as obtaining between predicates and arguments (i.e., between linguistic objects), they are actually relations that obtain in the world. I would rather, then, discard the term 'case' as a rubric under which to subsume such notions. Though it is common in current parlance to make statements like 'NP_i is the agent of the verb', it seems preferable to say 'NP_i refers to the agent of the action denoted by the verb'. One of the essential problems confronting syntactic theory is determining how a speaker of a language is able to obtain the kind of information expressed in the second kind of sentence, given certain structural information in the linguistic objects to be decoded. The notions Subject and Object as employed in this study may be viewed as playing a role in expressing the correct generalizations in this regard.

Suppose that we re-dub the so-called cases as 'w-relations', where w is meant to suggest 'world'. For each argument of each predicate in a sentence, we want to know what w-relations the argument's referent or referents enter into. One way of formalizing the means by which such knowledge is obtained is by associating with every predicate a set of statements each of which conforms to the schema

(1) $a(P)$ refers to $w_i(W)$

where a is a grammatical relation, w_i a w-relation, and W some action, event, state of affairs, or whatever to which the referent of $a(P)$ bears the relation w_i. Instances of the schema (1) as applied to individual predicates are as follows:

(2)   a. SUBJ*(run)* refers to AGENT(RUNNING)
      b. OBJ*(hit)* refers to PATIENT(HITTING)
      c. SUBJ*(like)* refers to EXPERIENCER(LIKING)

d. OBJ*(sadden)* refers to EXPERIENCER (SAD)

It is clear that in such statements SUBJ and OBJ have to be interpreted as 'Logical Subject/Object'; otherwise, incorrect claims would be made about sentences like

(3)   a. Maxine is liked by Harry.
      b. Republicans are saddened by recent history.

where the 'Surface Subject' (this notion corresponding roughly to our notion of 'unmarked argument') does not refer to the Experiencer in (3a) and does refer to the Experiencer in (3b). One could, of course, set up equivalence statements such as

(4)   Surface Subjects of passives correspond to Surface Objects
      of actives.

which is essentially what the passive transformation is supposed to do. But if we are attempting systematically to avoid a strategy of this type (as we are in developing a corepresentational theory), then the equation of SUBJ/OBJ with Logical Subject/Object seems necessary.

A final remark before leaving this topic concerns the problem of defining the terms 'Subject' and 'Object'. The difficulties in this regard have often been pointed out, and it might appear at first that they militate against making reference to such notions in a rigorously formulated theory of grammar. But the mere fact that a notion is difficult or impossible to define does not invalidate it if it is useful and intuitively accessible. Certain fundamental notions must be taken as primitives in any science: Within linguistics there are a variety of such notions, including 'sentence', 'predicate', 'constituent', and so on; in other fields, we might indicate such notions as 'point' and 'line' in geometry, 'mass' and 'gravity' in physics, 'plant' and 'animal' in biology, or 'space' in astronomy. I would argue, then, that our notions of Subject and Object need not be viewed as suspect solely because they cannot be defined. (It is worth pointing out that w-relations are not susceptible to hard and fast definitions either.)

6.3. Two Conceptions of Grammatical Theory

I conclude this study with some remarks on two different ways of viewing the theory of grammar, ways which I will call 'notionalist' (or 'conceptualist') and 'formalist'. The former perspective is dominant in traditional grammar and may be characterized as follows: The 'content system' of any language is presumed to be characterizable by reference to a universal system of categories and relations; a description of the grammatical structure of a sentence is then viewed as the assignment of various elements of the sentence to specific categories and the identification of significant relationships that may obtain among the categorially identified elements. The traditional sort of analysis which identifies 'parts of speech' and assigns elements of sentences to functional roles such as 'subject', 'predicate', 'complement', and so on is the embodiment of the notionalist perspective. As noted in §6.1, CORG may be viewed as an explicit theory of the foundations of this type of analysis.

The formalist perspective, which is not totally unrelated to the notionalist one, though its points of emphasis are quite different, has its origins in the distributionally oriented type of analysis associated with American structuralism and particularly with the approach identified with Zellig S. Harris. In syntax, what this perspective involves is a view of grammatical structure according to which the categories and relations of traditional grammar play a less important role, and grammatical description is seen to be concerned primarily with specifying patterns of occurrence and co-occurrence of elements. The main purpose of this type of analysis was to provide a method for representing the grammatical structure of sentences (and for discovering this structure) without invoking semantic criteria — the assumption being that insights about semantics would follow from the results of purely formal analysis, the independently constructed syntax then serving as a guide to the terra incognita of meaning. There are certain useful purposes to be served by this sort of analysis, and it is not my intent here to disparage or dismiss it. I do, however, wish to question its usefulness for certain purposes.

It was the formalist approach, as just characterized, that was inherited by Chomsky from his predecessors — Harris most particularly. While it was ultimately rejected by him in a number of its aspects, it none the less strongly influenced his thinking in certain ways. Indeed, I think that a case can be made for the position that TG is essentially a formalist approach, though the concerns of its adherents are frequently of a notional sort. What I wish to argue is that it is precisely the formalist nature of TG that has impeded the attainment of certain of its professed goals and that outright adoption of a notionalist perspective will hasten progress in some important research areas.[4]

To begin with, let us consider how the notion of grammatical transformations developed and what effects this had on linguists who chose to embrace the notion. As is well known, the theory of transformations grew out of Harris's attempts to develope a set of purely formal procedures for analyzing the structure of discourse. A major problem that presented itself in this regard was stylistic variation in grammatical form; since one of the components of Harris's method was the identification of 'equivalent' environments of elements, it was necessary to provide a principled way of neturalizing the effects of such things as variation in constituent order. For example, suppose that a discourse were to contain the sequence (5a) and later the sequence (5b):

(5) a. W now diagonalize matrix M . . .
     b. Matrix M having been diagonalized . . .

The environments of the expression *matrix M* are equivalent in an important sense, and yet the equivalence is not evident on purely formal grounds. Harris's solution to this problem was to provide a procedure for 'normalizing' texts such that all sylistic variants would be reduced to a single form. This in turn required that some criterion be provided for determining which kinds of variation were simply sylistic and which were not, and it was in this connection that the notion of co-occurrence equivalence (the basis for the original Harrisian conception of the transformational relationship) came to be an object of interest.

Consistent with his structuralist orientation, Harris worked without reference to meaning. A co-occurrence relation, for him, was defined as obtaining between elements in specified formal configurations, not as holding between elements on which some abstract relation such as Subject or Object was assumed to obtain. Let us consider the active-passive relation as a case in point. Suppose that V is a verb that can occur in both active and passive form; let $N(\,'V)$ denote 'N occurring to the left of V', and $N(V')$, 'N occurring to the right of V'. The following conditions hold if active and passive are compared:

(a) The ranges of $N(\,'V)$ in actives and $N(V')$ in passives are identical; that is, if some N can occur as $N(V')$ in a passive construction with V as its verb, whereas if it cannot occur as $N(\,'V)$ in the active, it also cannot occur as $N(V')$ in the passive.

(b) An analogous condition holds with regard to $N(V')$ in active and $N(\,'V)$ in passive.

Thus, V in both constructions maintains exactly the same range of possible co-occurences, the only difference between the two constructional types being the order of Ns with respect to V. There is then a clear and important sense in which the two constructions are equivalent, and a relation of equivalence based on co-occurence is thus defined between them — this relationship expressed by the passive transformation.

Chomsky argued for a passive transformation on somewhat different, though clearly related, grounds. In the context of a generative grammar, he suggested, failure to recognize a relationship between active and corresponding passive would lead to undue complication of the grammar. For example, for each verb it would be necessary to specify its co-occurrence valence twice, once for each order of Ns relative to it. That is, every verb would have to have associated with it a series of· statements of the form

(6)   a. $N(´V)$ obeys restriction R_1 in active
      b. $N(V´)$ obeys restriction R_2 in active
      c. $N(´V)$ obeys restriction R_2 in passive
      d. $N(V´)$ obeys restriction R_1 in passive

where R is a selectional (co-òccurrence) restriction. If, on the other hand, there is a transformation deriving one construction type from the other, or both from some third type, then specifications of co-occurrence properties of the type schematized in (6) can be cut in half. That is, R_1 and R_2 need be stated with respect to only one order of constituents, equivalent orders being derived via transformations (which are presumed to preserve co-occurrence structure).

As pointed out in Chapter 1, the approach just described is built on a tacit but critical assumption — namely, that facts about co-occurrence are to be accounted for 'concretely' in terms of formal cues such as relative order, rather than 'abstractly' in terms of 'notional' relations such as Subject and Object. This assumption, moreover, is the very embodiment of the formalist perspective. Given that this was the dominant viewpoint of the time, the Chomsky-Harris arguments for the recognition of transformations appear quite compelling; but once a notionalist perspective is countenanced as well, it becomes quite clear that the transformational solution to this particular problem (i.e., simplifying statements of co-occurrence restrictions by recognizing relationships such as that between active and corresponding passive) is not the only one available in principle.

In Chapter 1 we discussed some problems which could be neutralized within a CORG framework but which have presented some difficulties from a transformational point of view. These involved underlying constituent order and the treatment of certain types of agreement. If the conclusions drawn there are correct, then we would appear to have some substantive indication of the superiority of the notionalist perspective, at least for certain purposes. It is also worth pointing out that few transformalists have remained consistently true to formalist principles; much of the interest in TG that developed after its introduction by Harris and Chomsky was due to its usefulness as a formal tool for semantic analyses — and, indeed, much of the transformational literature of a certain vintage has something of the flavour of that portion of the philosophical literature which seeks to uncover the 'logical' form of statements in ordinary language, which form may be obscured by its 'grammatical' (i.e., surface) structure. But too often the interesting semantic questions were presumed unanswerable except in the context of a theory in which underlying representations had 'independent syntactic motivation' — the need for which was often presumed more for dogmatic reasons than for substantive ones, this presumption being the continued homage paid by TG to its formalist forebears. The main appeal of generative semantics, I suspect, stems from its legitimization of what most transformationalists were doing all along, i.e., a certain kind of semantic analysis couched in terms of a formalized theory of sound-meaning correlations of some apparent promise. Much of the work done along these lines has, however, the anomalous feel of essentially notionalist practice couched in a formalist theoretical framework.

The essential difference between the two perspectives is one of priorities. The formalist is primarily interested in distributional patterns, hoping that studying them for their own sake will reveal important facets of linguistic organization. The notionalist is primarily interested in correlations between manifest linguistic objects and their interpretations, seeing distributional generalizations only as consequences of the most viable theory of such correlations. It is my contention that the latter perspective is likely to be more useful for a variety of purposes than the former. Once the transformationalist notion of underlying (categorial) representation is replaced by the notion of relational representation, certain questions naturally arise: What general principles can be given for associating a given relational status with a particular manifest element? What kinds of relational interpretations are possible for sentences, and what kinds are not? In sentences where more than one predicate appears, how is it to be determined which elements are arguments of which predicates? What kind of objects can be arguments of predicates, and under what conditions? All of these questions have arisen in the course of this study, prompted by the assumption that the goal of a theory of grammar is to provide hypotheses as to correlations between manifest linguistic objects and certain features of their interpretations. Moreover, I would suggest that once these questions are raised, a completely new perspective is gained on some otherwise perplexing problems — e.g., those pertaining to finding an explanation of the facts covered by the Complex NP and Coordinate Structure Constraints. The entire conception of the domain problem, which is at the very heart of the concerns of this work, arises as a direct result of the questions raised above.

Let me hasten to add, however, that I do not mean to reject the view that FORMALIZATION of grammars is an essential part of the linguistic enterprise. As noted in the Prospectus, I have adopted this view, and I have sought to be consistent with it to the fullest possible extent. I also do not wish to claim that TG, which I have subjected to some sharp criticism on a variety of grounds, is necessarily worthless or uninteresting; it remains, in my view, of considerable value for both pedagogical and heuristic purposes — in much the same fashion as classical mechanics or Euclidean geometry. My claim is only that solutions of certain problems require a different point of view, the essentials of which I have sought to articulate here. In linguistics as elsewhere, necessity remains the mother of invention.

Notes

1. I am here making the assumption, probably unjustified, that the terms 'competence' and 'performance' in their current usages refer to coherent notions. I do so solely to facilitate discussion.
2. Actually, the parable is slightly oversimplified. In doing linguistic analysis, we presumably have access not only to outputs but to speaker intuitions. The intuitional component of linguistic data would, in the parable, be realizable as 'yes/no' statements on the part of the machine as to the inadmissibility of statements of the form $x + y = z$. To incorporate recognition of the intuitional component into the parable would, however, not change its force.
3. We are here identifying the notions 'grammar of L' and 'algorithm for generating L'. As pointed out in §1.2, it is not actually necessary to assume that generative (i.e. fully formalized) grammars are algorithms. Even if we assume, however, that grammars are non-algorithmic axiomatizations, the essential point remains unchanged; the language user cannot be automatically presumed to know even the most beautiful axiomatization characterizing his or her language.
4. This view has, of course, also been adopted by proponents of relational grammar.

REFERENCES

Bach, E. (1971). Questions. *Ling. Inq.* **2**, 153-66.

Bever, T. G. (1970). The cognitive basis for linguistic structures. In
J. R. Hayes (ed.), *Cognition and the Development of Language.*
New York: John Wiley and Sons. 279-362.

Cattell, R. (1976). Constraints on movement rules. *Lg.* **52**, 18-50.

Chomsky, N. (1957). *Syntactic Structures.* The Hague: Mouton and Co.

Emonds, J. E. (1970). Root and Structure-Preserving Transformations.
Mimeographed, Indiana University Linguistics Club.

Fillmore, C. J. (1968). The case for case. In E. Bach and R. T. Harms
(eds.), *Universals in Linguistic Theory.* New York: Holt, Rinehart, and
Winston, 1-90.

—— 1969. Toward a modern theory of case. In D. Reibel and S. A.
Schane (eds.), *Modern Studies in English.* Englewood Cliffs, N. J.:
Prentice-Hall, 361-76.

Grinder, J. and Postal, P. M. (1971). Missing antecedents. *Ling. Inq.*
2, 269-312.

Grosu, A. (1972). The Strategic Content of Island Constraints. Ohio
State University Working Papers in Linguistics. No. 13.

Hankamer, J. (1973). Unacceptable ambiguity. *Ling. Inq.* **4**, 17-68.

Hudson, G. (1972). Is deep structure linear? UCIA Papers in Syntax.
2, 51-77.

Hutchinson, L. G. (1974). Grammar as theory. In D. Cohen (ed.),
Explaining Linguistic Phenomena. New York: Halstead Press-
John Wiley and Sons, 43-74.

Iwamoto, K. (1974). Relativization in Japanese. Unpublished Paper,
University of Minnesota.

Jackendoff, R. S. (1972). *Semantic Interpretation in Generative
Grammar.* Cambridge, Mass.: MIT Press.

Johnson, D. E. (1976). Toward a Relationally Based Theory of Grammar.
Mimeographed, Indiana University Linguistics Club.

Kac, M. B. (1972a). Formal Aspects of Semantic Representation. UCLA
Dissertation.

——(1972b). A re-evaluation of some assumptions about constituent
structure. J. L. 92, 28-54.

——(1972c). On some empirical claims concerning the interaction of
VP-ellipsis and anaphora. UCLA Papers in Syntax. 1, 86-105.

——(1973). On a certain true generalization concerning English constituent order. Minnesota Working Papers in Linguistics and Philosophy of Language 1. 81-6.

——(1974a). Explanatory Adequacy and the Complex NP Constraint. Mimeographed, Indiana University Linguistics Club.

——(1974b). Autonomous linguistics and psycholinguistics. Minnesota Working Papers in Linguistics and Philosophy of Language 2. 42-8.

——(1976a). On composite predication in English. In M. Shibatani (ed.), *The Grammar of Causative Constructions* (Syntax and Semantics, Vol. 6). New York: Academic Press. 229-58.

——(1976). Hypothetical constructs in syntax. In J. Wirth (ed.), *Assessing Linguistic Arguments.* New York: Hemisphere Press-John Wiley and Sons.

Langacker, R. W. (1969). Pronominalization and the chain of command. In D. Reibel and S. A. Schane (eds.), *Modern Studies in English.* Englewood Cliffs, N. J.: Prentice-Hall. 160-86.

——(1974). Movement rules in functional perspective. *Lg.* **50.** 630-64.

Norman, L. J. (1974). Functional Relations in Natural Language. University of Minnesota Dissertation.

Perlmutter, D. M. (1971). *Deep and Surface Structure Constraints in Syntax.* New York: Holt, Rinehart, and Winston.

Peters, P. S. (1970). Why there are many universal bases. Papers in Linguistics 1. 27-43.

Ringen, C. O. (1972). On arguments for rule ordering. *Found. Lang.* 8, 266-73.

Rodman, R. (1971). A critical look at some movement constraints. UCLA Papers in Syntax 1. 106-60.

——(1973). Movement constraints on transformations that do not move elements. UCLA Papers in Syntax 3. 38-69.

Ross, J. R. (1967). Constraints on Variables in Syntax. MIT Dissertation.

——(1971). Gapping and the order of constituents. In M. Bierwisch and K. E. Heidolph (eds.), *Progress in Linguistics.* The Hague: Mouton and Co. 249-59.

Sanders, G. A. (1970). Invariant Ordering. Mimeographed, Indiana University Linguistics Club.

Schachter, P. (1973). Focus and relativization. *Lg.* 19-46.

INDEX

ABOUT THE BOOK AND AUTHOR

This monograph in linguistics presents a nontransformational model of generative grammar called corepresentational grammar. A corepresentational description of a language consists of a set of principles on the basis of which information pertaining to abstract relations among elements of a sentence may be extracted directly from surface structure. The resulting theory provides solutions to a variety of problems pertaining to word order, complementation, complex nominals, and coordinate structures.

Michael B. Kac is an associate professor of linguistics at the University of Minnesota.